Workbook

Science

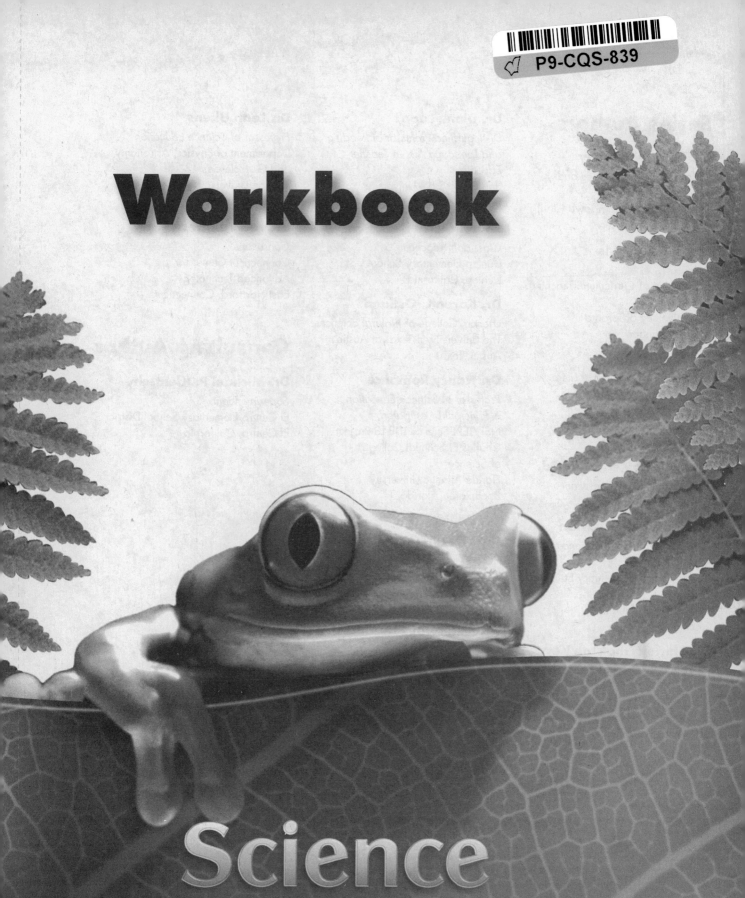

PEARSON
Scott Foresman

Editorial Offices: Glenview, Illinois • Parsippany, New Jersey • New York, New York
Sales Offices: Needham, Massachusetts • Duluth, Georgia • Glenview, Illinois
Coppell, Texas • Sacramento, California • Mesa, Arizona

www.sfsuccessnet.com

Series Authors

Dr. Timothy Cooney
Professor of Earth Science and Science Education
University of Northern Iowa (UNI)
Cedar Falls, Iowa

Dr. Jim Cummins
Professor
Department of Curriculum, Teaching, and Learning
The University of Toronto
Toronto, Canada

Dr. James Flood
Distinguished Professor of Literacy and Language
School of Teacher Education
San Diego State University
San Diego, California

Barbara Kay Foots, M.Ed.
Science Education Consultant
Houston, Texas

Dr. M. Jenice Goldston
Associate Professor of Science Education
Department of Elementary Education Programs
University of Alabama
Tuscaloosa, Alabama

Dr. Shirley Gholston Key
Associate Professor of Science Education
Instruction and Curriculum Leadership Department College of Education
University of Memphis
Memphis, Tennessee

Dr. Diane Lapp
Distinguished Professor of Reading and Language Arts in Teacher Education
San Diego State University
San Diego, California

Sheryl Mercier
Classroom Teacher
Dunlap Elementary School
Dunlap, California

Dr. Karen L. Ostlund
UTeach, College of Natural Sciences
The University of Texas at Austin
Austin, Texas

Dr. Nancy Romance
Professor of Science Education & Principal Investigator
NSF/IERI Science IDEAS Project
Charles E. Schmidt College of Science
Florida Atlantic University
Boca Raton, Florida

Dr. William Tate
Chair and Professor of Education and Applied Statistics
Department of Education
Washington University
St. Louis, Missouri

Dr. Kathryn C. Thornton
Professor
School of Engineering and Applied Science
University of Virginia
Charlottesville, Virginia

Dr. Leon Ukens
Professor of Science Education
Department of Physics, Astronomy, and Geosciences
Towson University
Towson, Maryland

Steve Weinberg
Consultant
Connecticut Center for Advanced Technology
East Hartford, Connecticut

Consulting Author

Dr. Michael P. Klentschy
Superintendent
El Centro Elementary School District
El Centro, California

ISBN: 0-328-12611-X
ISBN: 0-328-20065-4

3 4 5 6 7 8 9 10 V084 13 12 11 10 09 08 07 06 05

Unit A
Life Science

Unit B
Earth Science

Unit C
Physical Science

Unit D
Space and Technology

GRADE 2 WORKBOOK

Illustration Credits

167 Big Sesh Studios
172 Bob Kayganich

Photo Credits

Every effort has been made to secure permission and provide appropriate credit for photographic material. The publisher deeply regrets any omission and pledges to correct errors called to its attention in subsequent editions.
Unless otherwise acknowledged, all photographs are the property of Scott Foresman, a division of Pearson Education.
Photo locators denoted as follows: Top (T), Center (C), Bottom (B), Left (L), Right (R) Background (Bkgd)

161 Steve Kaufman/Corbis, ©OSF/Animals Animals/Earth Scenes
162 Joe McDonald/Corbis, © George D.Lepp/Corbis, Getty Images, ©Tom Brakefield/Corbis
163 Corbis, Joe McDonald/Corbis, W. Perry Conway/Corbis, William Bernard/Corbis
164 Jonathan Blair/Corbis, ©Soames Summerhays/Photo Researchers, Inc., ©DK Images
166 ©Sam Abell/NGS Image Collection
167 ©DK Images
171 ©DK Images
172 ©Giulio Andreini, Corbis

Name ______________________________

Use with Chapter 1.

Draw a picture or write a sentence to go with each word.

flower	environment
leaves	stem
nutrients	adapted
roots	prairie

Directions: Read the words and draw pictures to illustrate them or write sentences about them. Cut out the boxes to use as word cards.
Home Activity: Ask your child to identify the words that name parts of a plant *(flower, leaf, roots, stem)* and then explain how *roots* and *nutrients, adapt* and *environment,* and *environment* and *prairie* are related.

Name ______________________________

Use with Chapter 1.

Predict

Read the science story.

Pine Cones

Pine trees do not grow flowers. They grow cones. Their seeds grow inside the cones. When the seeds are ready, the cones open and the seeds drop out of the cones. The seeds fall to the ground.

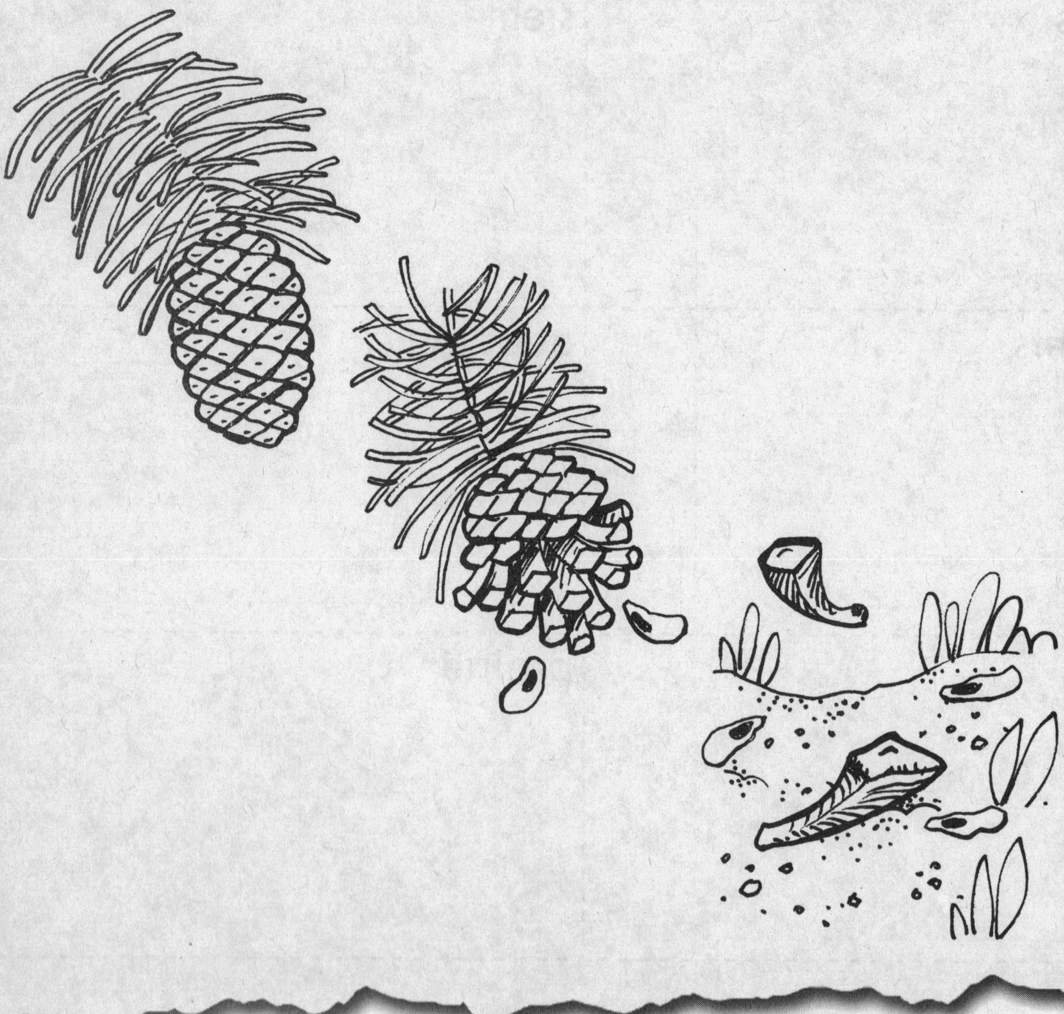

Name ______________________________

Use with Chapter 1.

Apply It!

Predict what will happen to the pine tree seeds next. Fill in the graphic organizer.

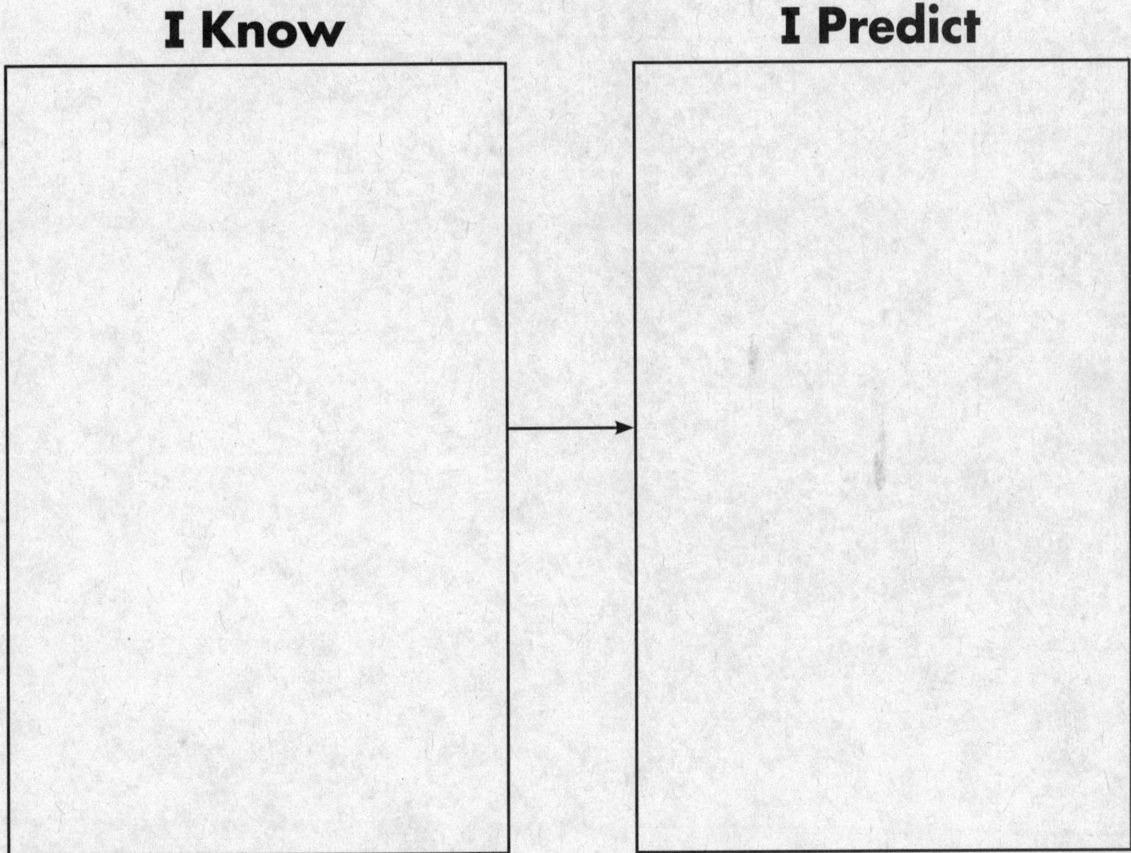

Directions: Read the Science Story and look at the pictures. Think about what you know about seeds and plants and write those facts in the *I know* box. Then write your prediction in the *I predict* box.
Home Activity: Your child learned about predicting. Put a pot of water on the stove and turn on the burner. Ask your child to predict what will happen to the water. Discuss how your child used what he or she knows about stoves and water to predict.

Notes

Name ____________________

Use with pages 7–9.

What are the parts of a plant?

Before You Read Lesson 1

Read each sentence. Do you think it is true? Do you think it is not true? Circle the word or words after each sentence that tell what you think.

1. Plants get water and nutrients from the soil.	True	Not True
2. Roots make food for the plant.	True	Not True
3. The stem is one of the main parts of a plant.	True	Not True

After You Read Lesson 1

Read each sentence again. Circle the word or words after each sentence that tell what you think now. Did you change any answers? Put an **X** by each answer that you changed.

1. Plants get water and nutrients from the soil.	True	Not True
2. Roots make food for the plant.	True	Not True
3. The stem is one of the main parts of a plant.	True	Not True

Home Activity: Together talk about your child's answers. Have your child explain why his or her answers may have changed after reading the lesson.

Name ______________________________

Use with pages 7–9.

Complete the Sentence

Write the word that completes each sentence.

roots	nutrients	leaves	flower

1. Plant parts that grow down in soil are ____________.

2. A colorful plant part that makes seeds is a ____________.

3. Plant parts that take in sunshine and air are ____________.

4. To live and grow, living things need ____________.

Predict

5. Draw a picture to predict what will happen next.

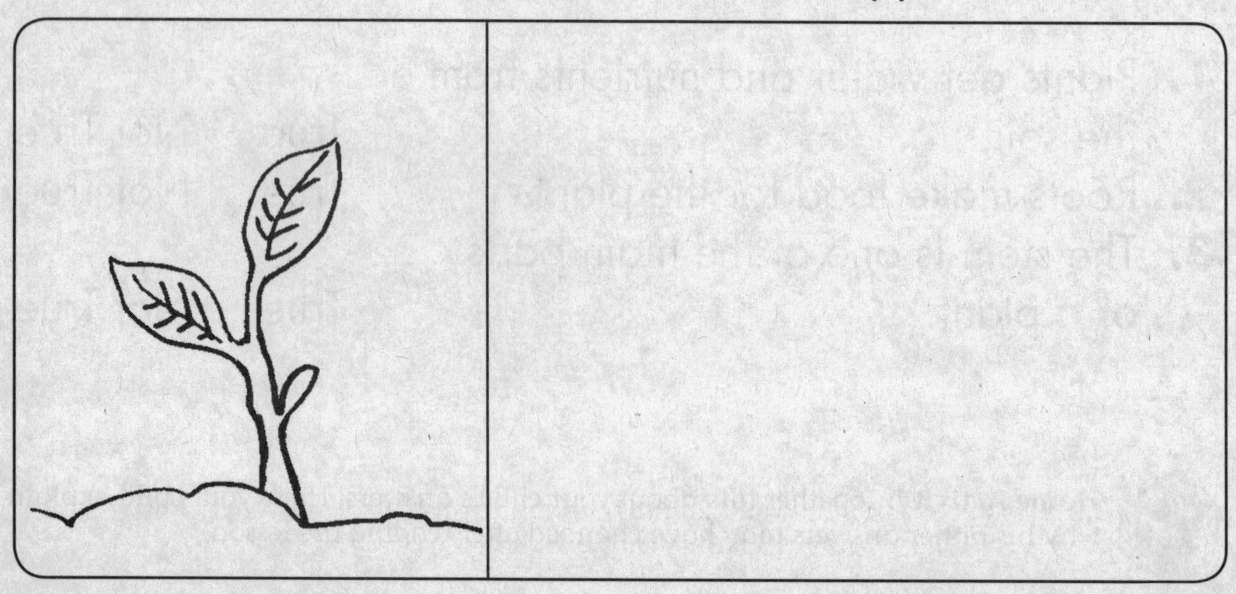

Name ________________________________

Use with pages 10–11.

How are seeds scattered?

Before You Read Lesson 2

Read each sentence. Do you think it is true? Do you think it is not true? Circle the word or words after each sentence that tell what you think.

1.	*Scatter* means "to break into small pieces."	True	Not True
2.	Seeds grow inside of fruits.	True	Not True
3.	Air and water can carry seeds to new places.	True	Not True

After You Read Lesson 2

Read each sentence again. Circle the word or words after each sentence that tell what you think now. Did you change any answers? Put an **X** by each answer that you changed.

1.	*Scatter* means "to break into small pieces."	True	Not True
2.	Seeds grow inside of fruits.	True	Not True
3.	Air and water can carry seeds to new places.	True	Not True

Home Activity: Together talk about your child's answers. Have your child explain why his or her answers may have changed after reading the lesson.

Name ____________________________

Complete the Sentence

Write the word that completes each sentence.

scatter	cover	seeds	fruits

1. Many new plants grow from ____________.

2. When you spread out something, you ____________ it.

3. Fruits ____________ and protect seeds.

4. Some ____________ get stuck on the fur of animals.

Predict

5. Draw a picture to show how the fruit will travel.

Fruit	Way of Traveling
burr	
maple fruit	

Name ________________________________

Use with pages 12–15.

How are plants grouped?

Before You Read Lesson 3

Read each sentence. Do you think it is true? Do you think it is not true? Circle the word or words after each sentence that tell what you think.

1. All plants have flowers.	True	Not True
2. Plants with flowers grow only in gardens.	True	Not True
3. Some seeds grow inside cones.	True	Not True
4. Some plants do not make seeds.	True	Not True

After You Read Lesson 3

Read each sentence again. Circle the word or words after each sentence that tell what you think now. Did you change any answers? Put an **X** by each answer that you changed.

1. All plants have flowers.	True	Not True
2. Plants with flowers grow only in gardens.	True	Not True
3. Some seeds grow inside cones.	True	Not True
4. Some plants do not make seeds.	True	Not True

Home Activity: Together talk about your child's answers. Have your child explain why his or her answers may have changed after reading the lesson.

Name ______________________________

Lesson 3 Review

Use with pages 12–15.

Complete the Sentence

Write the word that completes each sentence.

flowers	plants	seeds	two

1. Plants can be grouped into ______________ kinds.

2. One kind of plant has ______________.

3. Trees are ______________.

4. Ferns do not make ______________.

Infer

5. Color the picture that shows what will grow from this pine cone.

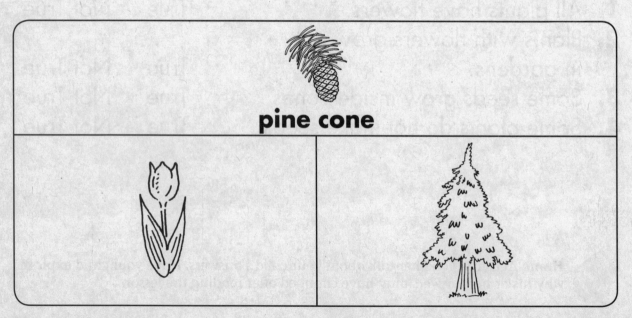

pine cone

Name ______________________

Use with pages 16–19.

How are some woodland plants adapted?

Before You Read Lesson 4

Read each sentence. Do you think it is true? Do you think it is not true? Circle the word or words after each sentence that tell what you think.

1.	Plants live in many different places.	True	Not True
2.	Only trees live in a woodland.	True	Not True
3.	Plants can adapt to live in a cold or wet place.	True	Not True

After You Read Lesson 4

Read each sentence again. Circle the word or words after each sentence that tell what you think now. Did you change any answers? Put an **X** by each answer that you changed.

1.	Plants live in many different places.	True	Not True
2.	Only trees live in a woodland.	True	Not True
3.	Plants can adapt to live in a cold or wet place.	True	Not True

Home Activity: Together talk about your child's answers. Have your child explain why his or her answers may have changed after reading the lesson.

Name ______________________________

Use with pages 16–19.

Complete the Sentence

Write the word that completes each sentence.

adapted	rivers	flat	environment

1. The things around a plant are its ____________.

2. Living things have ______________ to their environment.

3. Maple trees have large ______________ leaves.

4. Some plants live near ______________.

Predict

5. Draw a picture to predict what will happen next.

Name ______________________

Use with pages 20–21.

How are some prairie plants adapted?

Before You Read Lesson 5

Read each sentence. Do you think it is true? Do you think it is not true? Circle the word or words after each sentence that tell what you think.

1.	A prairie has lots of trees and a little grass.	True	Not True
2.	Summers on a prairie can be hot and dry.	True	Not True
3.	Prairie plants have adapted to keep the water they need.	True	Not True

After You Read Lesson 5

Read each sentence again. Circle the word or words after each sentence that tell what you think now. Did you change any answers? Put an **X** by each answer that you changed.

1.	A prairie has lots of trees and a little grass.	True	Not True
2.	Summers on a prairie can be hot and dry.	True	Not True
3.	Prairie plants have adapted to keep the water they need.	True	Not True

Home Activity: Together talk about your child's answers. Have your child explain why his or her answers may have changed after reading the lesson.

Name ______________________________

Use with pages 20–21.

Complete the Sentence

Write the word that completes each sentence.

hot	environment	adapted	prairie

1. A place with lots of grass but not many trees is a ______________.

2. Many kinds of plants live in a prairie ______________.

3. Many prairies have very ______________ summers.

4. Some prairie plants are ______________ to keep water.

Picture Clues

5. Color the picture that shows the weather the prairie usually has.

Name ______________________________

Use with pages 22–23.

How are some desert plants adapted?

Before You Read Lesson 6

Read each sentence. Do you think it is true? Do you think it is not true? Circle the word or words after each sentence that tell what you think.

1.	Deserts are very dry.	True	Not True
2.	Desert plants do not need water.	True	Not True
3.	A cactus holds water in its stem.	True	Not True

After You Read Lesson 6

Read each sentence again. Circle the word or words after each sentence that tell what you think now. Did you change any answers? Put an **X** by each answer that you changed.

1.	Deserts are very dry.	True	Not True
2.	Desert plants do not need water.	True	Not True
3.	A cactus holds water in its stem.	True	Not True

Home Activity: Together talk about your child's answers. Have your child explain why his or her answers may have changed after reading the lesson.

Name ______________________________

Use with pages 22–23.

Complete the Sentence

Write the word that completes each sentence.

adapted	environment	night	deserts

1. Many ____________ are sunny and hot during the day.
2. Deserts can be cool at ____________.
3. Many different plants grow in a desert ____________.
4. Some desert plants are ____________ to hold water for a long time.

Infer

5. Draw one plant that could grow in the desert and one plant that could not.

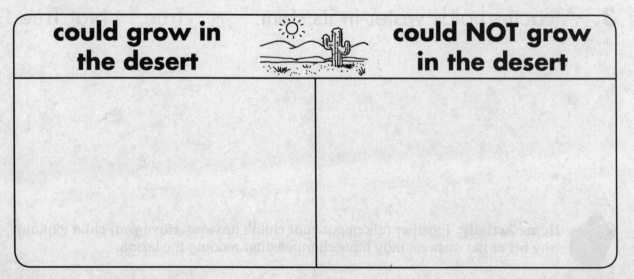

could grow in the desert	 could NOT grow in the desert

Name ______________________________

Use with pages 24–25.

How are some marsh plants adapted?

Before You Read Lesson 7

Read each sentence. Do you think it is true? Do you think it is not true? Circle the word or words after each sentence that tell what you think.

1. Some marsh plants get nutrients from water. True Not True
2. Some marsh plants get nutrients from insects. True Not True
3. The soil in a marsh has all the nutrients plants need. True Not True

After You Read Lesson 7

Read each sentence again. Circle the word or words after each sentence that tell what you think now. Did you change any answers? Put an **X** by each answer that you changed.

1. Some marsh plants get nutrients from water. True Not True
2. Some marsh plants get nutrients from insects. True Not True
3. The soil in a marsh has all the nutrients plants need. True Not True

Home Activity: Together talk about your child's answers. Have your child explain why his or her answers may have changed after reading the lesson.

Name ______________________

Lesson 7 Review

Use with pages 24–25.

Complete the Sentence

Write the word that completes each sentence.

adapted	marsh	nutrients	environment

1. A ______________ is an environment that is very wet.

2. Many kinds of plants grow in a marsh ______________.

3. The soil in a marsh may not have the ______________ that plants need.

4. Cattails are ______________ to grow in soil that has a lot of water.

Predict

5. Draw a picture to predict what will happen if this insect lands on a sundew plant.

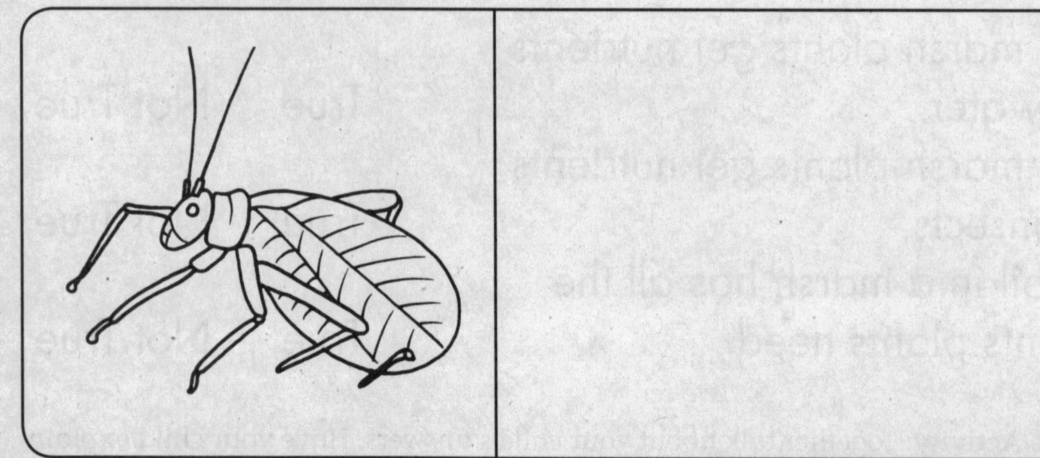

Name ______________________________

Use with Chapter 1.

Making Patterns

Anna collected maple and beech leaves.
She arranged the leaves in two patterns.

Here is how Anna arranged the leaves.

Use what you know about Anna's patterns.
Predict what two leaves Anna will add next.
Draw two more leaves in each pattern.

Directions: Look closely at Anna's patterns. Note what the pattern is and when it repeats. Then draw the next two leaves in each pattern.
Home Activity: Your child learned about patterns. After your child explains how he or she continued the patterns on the page, use pennies and nickels to make two patterns like the leaf patterns.

Notes

Family Science Activity

Make a Leaf Guide

Materials:
- White drawing paper
- Construction paper
- Pen or pencil
- Colored pens or markers
- Stapler

Steps
1. Look for plants that have leaves, inside and outside the house.
2. Ask your child to copy a leaf from each plant on a separate sheet of drawing paper. You can also pick the leaves and have your child trace their shapes.
3. Encourage your child to observe each leaf carefully. Talk about what each leaf looks like. Have your child add more details to each drawing. Then ask your child to color in the drawing with the appropriate colors.
4. Help your child identify each leaf. Label each drawing, telling the name of the plant each leaf comes from.
5. Make a cover on a sheet of construction paper for the leaf guide.
6. Help your child staple together the drawings of leaves and the cover to make the leaf guide.
7. Have your child show the leaf guide to someone who lives nearby. Talk about the different leaves and plants you can find where you live.

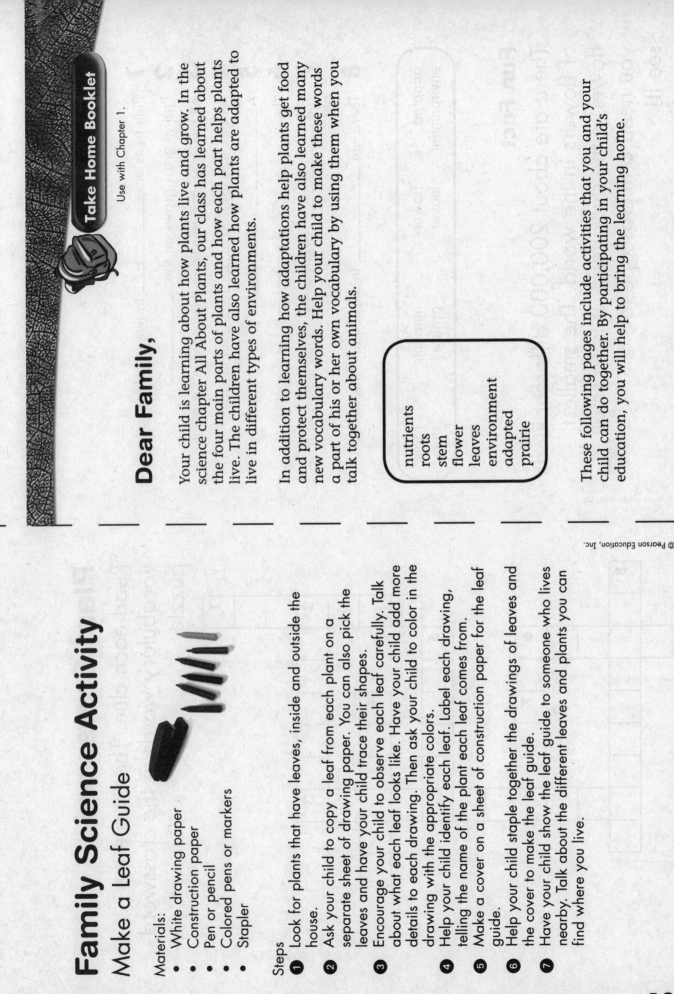

Take Home Booklet

Use with Chapter 1.

Dear Family,

Your child is learning about how plants live and grow. In the science chapter All About Plants, our class has learned about the four main parts of plants and how each part helps plants live. The children have also learned how plants are adapted to live in different types of environments.

In addition to learning how adaptations help plants get food and protect themselves, the children have also learned many new vocabulary words. Help your child to make these words a part of his or her own vocabulary by using them when you talk together about animals.

nutrients
roots
stem
flower
leaves
environment
adapted
prairie

These following pages include activities that you and your child can do together. By participating in your child's education, you will help to bring the learning home.

Clues

1 Pine trees are ____________ to live in cold weather.

2 Prairie grass grows on the ____________.

3 All the living and nonliving things around a plant.

4 An oak tree loses its ____________ in the fall.

5 A ____________ makes seeds.

6 The ____________ of a plant grow in the soil.

7 The ____________ carries water to the leaves of a plant.

8 There are ____________ in the soil and the water.

adapted	flower	nutrients	roots
environment	leaves	prairie	stem

Fun Fact

There are about 200,000 different kinds of flowers in the world. The smallest flower is the duckweed. It is so small you need a microscope to see it!

Plant Crossword

Read each clue. Then write the vocabulary words in the crossword puzzle.

Name ___________________________

Use with Chapter 2.

Draw a picture or write a sentence to go with each word.

reptile	mammal
bird	amphibian
fish	camouflage
gills	insect

Directions: Read the words and draw pictures to illustrate them or write sentences about them. Cut out the boxes to use as word cards.
Home Activity: Review the word cards *reptile, bird, fish, mammal, amphibian,* and *insect* with your child. Look through magazines together. Help your child find an example of each kind of animal.

Name ______________________________

Use with page 37.

Alike and Different

Read the science article. Fill in the chart. Tell how honey bees and spiders are alike and different.

Honey Bees and Spiders

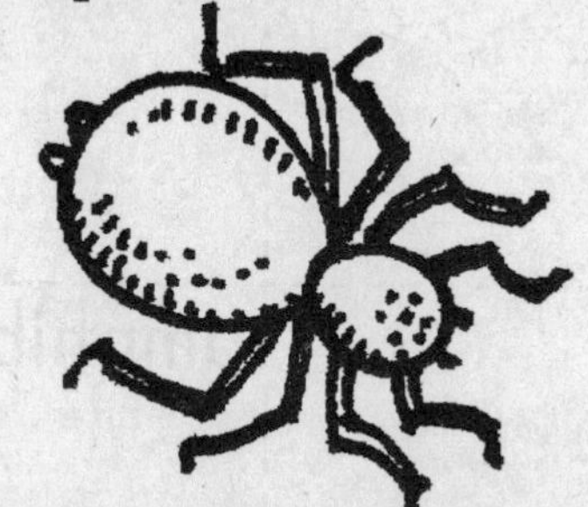

Honey bees do not have bones. They have three body parts and six legs. They have wings. They can walk and fly.

Spiders do not have bones. They have two body parts and eight legs. They cannot fly. They do not have wings. They walk.

Apply It!

Use the chart on the next page. Tell how a honey bee and spider are alike and different.

Name ______________________________

Use with page 37.

Alike	Different

Directions: Read the science article. Think about how honey bees and spiders are alike. Write your ideas in the chart under *Alike*. Then think about how honey bees and spiders are different. Write your ideas in the chart under *Different*.
Home Activity: Your child learned about the concept of alike and different. Find pictures of two different animals in a magazine. Discuss with your child how the animals are alike and different.

Notes

Name ______________________

Use with pages 39–41.

What are some animals with backbones?

Before You Read Lesson 1

Read each sentence. Do you think it is true? Do you think it is not true? Circle the word or words after each sentence that tell what you think.

1. Mammals are one group of animals with bones. True Not True

2. Only birds hatch from eggs. True Not True

3. Both fish and reptiles have scales. True Not True

4. Amphibians do not have bones. True Not True

After You Read Lesson 1

Read each sentence again. Circle the word or words after each sentence that tell what you think now. Did you change any answers? Put an **X** by each answer that you changed.

1. Mammals are one group of animals with bones. True Not True

2. Only birds hatch from eggs. True Not True

3. Both fish and reptiles have scales. True Not True

4. Amphibians do not have bones. True Not True

Home Activity: Together talk about your child's answers. Have your child explain why his or her answers may have changed after reading the lesson.

Name ______________________________

Use with pages 39–41.

Complete the Sentence

Write the word that completes each sentence.

birds	fish	reptiles	amphibian

1. Animals with scales and dry skin are ____________.
2. Animals with feathers and wings are ____________.
3. Animals with smooth, wet skin are ____________.
4. Animals with fins for swimming are ____________.

Alike and Different

5. Write two ways that a bird and a fish are alike and two ways they are different.

	Alike	Different

Name ______________________

Use with pages 42–43.

What are some ways mammals are adapted?

Before You Read Lesson 2

Read each sentence. Do you think it is true? Do you think it is not true? Circle the word or words after each sentence that tell what you think.

1. Mammals can change to live in their environment. True Not True
2. Camouflage is all the living and nonliving things around an animal. True Not True
3. A mule deer's fur changes color from brown in summer to gray in winter. True Not True

After You Read Lesson 2

Read each sentence again. Circle the word or words after each sentence that tell what you think now. Did you change any answers? Put an **X** by each answer that you changed.

1. Mammals can change to live in their environment. True Not True
2. Camouflage is all the living and nonliving things around an animal. True Not True
3. A mule deer's fur changes color from brown in summer to gray in winter. True Not True

Home Activity: Together talk about your child's answers. Have your child explain why his or her answers may have changed after reading the lesson.

Name ______________________________

Use with pages 42–43.

Complete the Sentence

Write the word that completes each sentence.

sleep	environment	camouflage	adapted

1. The living and nonliving things around an animal are its ______________.

2. Animals have ______________ to live in their environments.

3. A color or shape that makes an animal hard to see is ______________.

4. Some animals ______________ for part of each winter.

Picture Clues

5. Color this picture so that the fish is camouflaged in its environment.

Name ______________________________

Use with pages 44–45.

What are some ways birds are adapted?

Before You Read Lesson 3

Read each sentence. Do you think it is true? Do you think it is not true? Circle the word or words after each sentence that tell what you think.

1. All birds use their wings to fly. True Not True
2. Some birds use camouflage to hide in their environment. True Not True
3. A hummingbird's beak is adapted for sipping liquid from flowers. True Not True

After You Read Lesson 3

Read each sentence again. Circle the word or words after each sentence that tell what you think now. Did you change any answers? Put an **X** by each answer that you changed.

1. All birds use their wings to fly. True Not True
2. Some birds use camouflage to hide in their environment. True Not True
3. A hummingbird's beak is adapted for sipping liquid from flowers. True Not True

Home Activity: Together talk about your child's answers. Have your child explain why his or her answers may have changed after reading the lesson.

Name ______________________

Lesson 3 Review

Use with pages 44–45.

Complete the Sentence

Write the word that completes each sentence.

penguin	wings	food	fly

1. Wings and feathers show that many birds are adapted to ______________.

2. A ______________ has special feathers that help it live in cold climates.

3. A hummingbird has a long, thin beak that helps it get ______________.

4. A bird's ______________ help it fly or swim.

Infer

5. Color the correct environment for a penguin.

Name ___________________________________

Use with pages 46–47.

What are some ways fish are adapted?

Before You Read Lesson 4

Read each sentence. Do you think it is true? Do you think it is not true? Circle the word or words after each sentence that tell what you think.

1. Gills and fins help fish live in the water. True Not True
2. Gills are body parts that help fish swim. True Not True
3. Some fish can change their shape to protect themselves. True Not True

After You Read Lesson 4

Read each sentence again. Circle the word or words after each sentence that tell what you think now. Did you change any answers? Put an **X** by each answer that you changed.

1. Gills and fins help fish live in the water. True Not True
2. Gills are body parts that help fish swim. True Not True
3. Some fish can change their shape to protect themselves. True Not True

Home Activity: Together talk about your child's answers. Have your child explain why his or her answers may have changed after reading the lesson.

Name ____________________

Use with pages 46–47.

Complete the Sentence

Write the word that completes each sentence.

gills	fins	spikes	feelers

1. Body parts that pull oxygen from the water are ____________.

2. Body parts that help fish swim are ____________.

3. Body parts that protect some fish from other animals are ____________.

4. Body parts that help some fish find food are ____________.

Predict

5. Draw three fish and show how each has adapted to living in water.

Name ____________________

Use with pages 48–49.

What are some ways reptiles are adapted?

Before You Read Lesson 5

Read each sentence. Do you think it is true? Do you think it is not true? Circle the word or words after each sentence that tell what you think.

1. Reptiles get cold when the air is cold and warm when the air is warm. True Not True
2. A chameleon uses its long, sticky tongue to catch food. True Not True
3. Snakes use teeth to chew their food. True Not True

After You Read Lesson 5

Read each sentence again. Circle the word or words after each sentence that tell what you think now. Did you change any answers? Put an **X** by each answer that you changed.

1. Reptiles get cold when the air is cold and warm when the air is warm. True Not True
2. A chameleon uses its long, sticky tongue to catch food. True Not True
3. Snakes use teeth to chew their food. True Not True

Home Activity: Together talk about your child's answers. Have your child explain why his or her answers may have changed after reading the lesson.

Name ______________________________

Use with pages 48–49.

Complete the Sentence

Write the word that completes each sentence.

air	light	warm	cold

1. Reptiles are adapted to changes in ______________ temperature.

2. Reptiles' bodies are ______________ when the air is cold.

3. A desert iguana's ______________ skin helps it keep cool.

4. Reptiles can move quickly when they are ______________.

Alike and Different

5. Write two ways that a snake and a turtle are alike and two ways they are different.

	Alike	Different

Name ______________________

Use with pages 50–51.

What are some ways amphibians are adapted?

Before You Read Lesson 6

Read each sentence. Do you think it is true? Do you think it is not true? Circle the word or words after each sentence that tell what you think.

1. Amphibians live in the water and on land. True Not True

2. Most amphibians have dry, rough skin. True Not True

3. Toads are amphibians. True Not True

After You Read Lesson 6

Read each sentence again. Circle the word or words after each sentence that tell what you think now. Did you change any answers? Put an **X** by each answer that you changed.

1. Amphibians live in the water and on land. True Not True

2. Most amphibians have dry, rough skin. True Not True

3. Toads are amphibians. True Not True

Home Activity: Together talk about your child's answers. Have your child explain why his or her answers may have changed after reading the lesson.

Name ______________________________

Use with pages 50–51.

Complete the Sentence

Write the word that completes each sentence.

heat	frog	night	water

1. Most amphibians are born in ______________.

2. The smooth, wet skin of a ______________ helps it live in moist environments.

3. Many toads stay away from sunlight and ______________.

4. Toads look for food at ______________.

Alike and Different

5. Write one way that a frog and a toad are alike and one way they are different.

	Alike	Different

Name ______________________

Use with pages 52–53.

What are some animals without backbones?

Before You Read Lesson 7

Read each sentence. Do you think it is true? Do you think it is not true? Circle the word or words after each sentence that tell what you think.

1. Most kinds of animals have bones. True Not True
2. Insects are one group of animals that do not have bones. True Not True
3. An octopus uses suction cups on its arms to hold its food. True Not True
4. Like beetles, spiders have six legs and no bones. True Not True

After You Read Lesson 7

Read each sentence again. Circle the word or words after each sentence that tell what you think now. Did you change any answers? Put an **X** by each answer that you changed.

1. Most kinds of animals have bones. True Not True
2. Insects are one group of animals that do not have bones. True Not True
3. An octopus uses suction cups on its arms to hold its food. True Not True
4. Like beetles, spiders have six legs and no bones. True Not True

Home Activity: Together talk about your child's answers. Have your child explain why his or her answers may have changed after reading the lesson.

Name ______________________________

Use with pages 52–55.

Complete the Sentence

Write the word that completes each sentence.

Insects	three	Antennae	octopus

1. ______________ are animals that do not have bones.

2. Insects have ______________ body parts.

3. ______________ help insects feel, smell, hear, and taste things.

4. An ______________ is an animal with suction cups on its arms.

Alike and Different

5. Write one way that a walkingstick and an ant are alike and one way they are different.

	Alike	Different

Name ________________________________

Use with pages 58–59.

Sorting Animals

Sort these animals into two groups—animals with bones and animals without bones. Color the graph to show how many animals you put in each group.

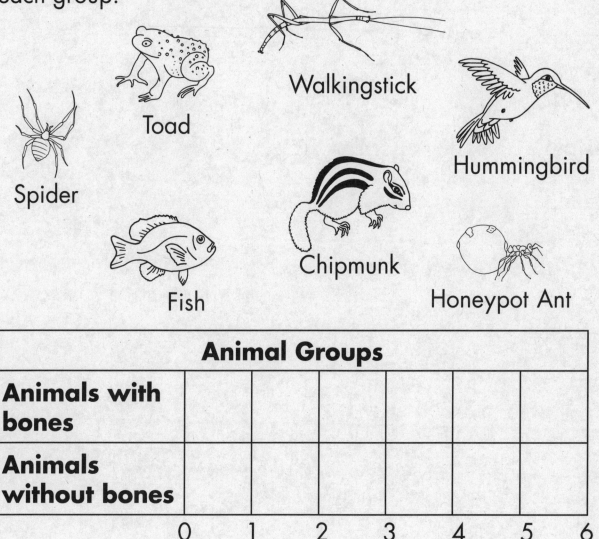

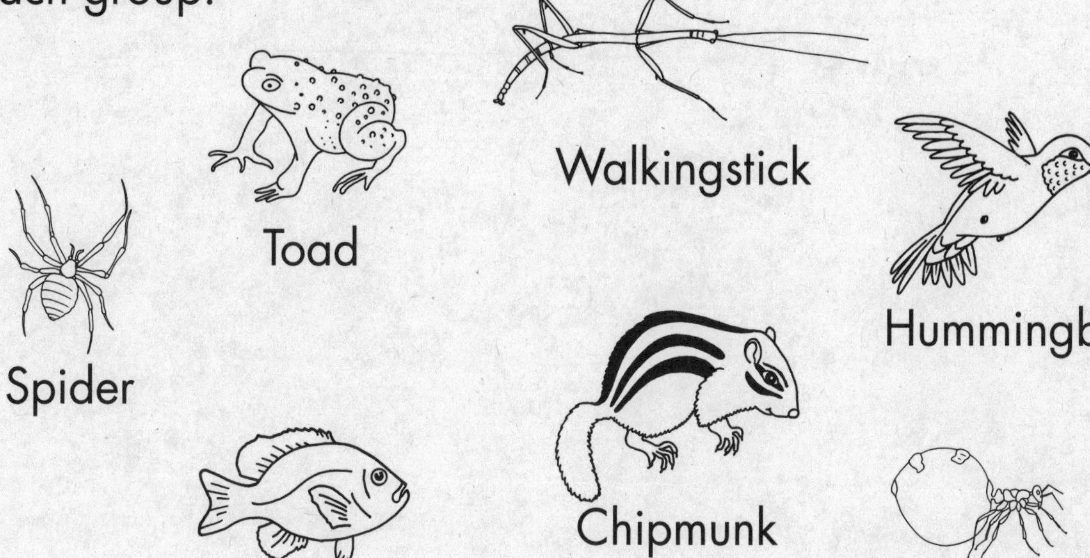

Animal Groups						
Animals with bones						
Animals without bones						
	0	1	2	3	4	5 6

Directions: Decide whether each animal shown on the page is an animal with bones or an animal without bones. (You can look in your book if you need help.) Find the correct row on the graph. Color one box in that row for the animal.
Home Activity: Your child learned how to fill in a graph. Ask your child to explain how he or she filled in the graph on the page. Then together make another graph for the same animals showing how many have fur or feathers and how many do not.

Notes

Family Science Activity

Polar Bear Camouflage

Materials:
- Colored construction paper
- White drawing paper
- Pen or pencil
- Scissors
- Glue

Steps

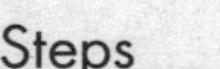

1. Talk about camouflage. Camouflage is when the color or shape of an animal makes it blend into its environment. Talk about how camouflage can help an animal.
2. Have your child draw two pictures of a bear shape on white paper. The drawings should only be the outline of the bear.
3. Cut out the bear drawings.
4. Glue one bear on colored paper. Glue the other bear on white paper. Ask your child which bear is easier to see.
5. Talk about how hard it is to see the white bear on the white paper. Explain that this is just like the natural camouflage of a polar bear in its habitat. The bear is white and it lives in a snowy environment. Talk about how the polar bear's adaptation can help it survive.

Take Home Booklet

Use with Chapter 2.

Dear Family,

Your child is learning about different groups of animals and their characteristics. In the science chapter All About Animals, our class has learned how different animals have adapted to their habitats. The children have also learned how these adaptations help animals to find food and protect themselves.

In addition to learning how different kinds of animals live in different environments, the children have also learned many new vocabulary words. Help your child to make these words a part of his or her own vocabulary by using them when you talk together about animals.

mammal
bird
fish
reptile
amphibian
insect
gills
camouflage

These following pages include activities that you and your child can do together. By participating in your child's education, you will help to bring the learning home.

Draw lines to match each picture with the kind of animal.

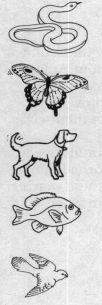

Amphibian

Reptile

Mammal

Bird

Fish

Insect

Fun Fact

A chameleon is a reptile. It has a very long tongue. Its tongue is even longer than its body! It uses its tongue to catch food. Imagine if your tongue was even longer than your body!

Literacy and Art

What is your favorite animal? What does it look like? Where does it live? What type of animal is it? Draw a picture of the animal in the box below. Then, write 2 or 3 details about the animal.

Name ___________________________

Vocabulary Preview

Use with Chapter 3.

Draw a picture or write a sentence to go with each word.

producer	prey
consumer	food chain
predator	food web

Directions: Read the words and draw pictures to illustrate them or write sentences about them. Cut out the boxes to use as word cards.
Home Activity: Pair the words *producer/consumer, predator/prey,* and *food chain/ food web* and ask your child to explain how the two words are related to each other.

Name ______________________________

Use with Chapter 3.

Cause and Effect

Look at the pictures.
Read the paragraph.
Answer the questions.

Science Activity

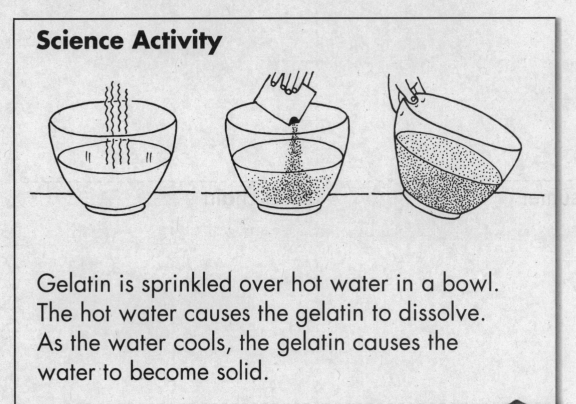

Gelatin is sprinkled over hot water in a bowl. The hot water causes the gelatin to dissolve. As the water cools, the gelatin causes the water to become solid.

Name ___________________________

Use with Chapter 3.

Apply It!

Infer What would happen to the water without the gelatin? Fill in the chart below.

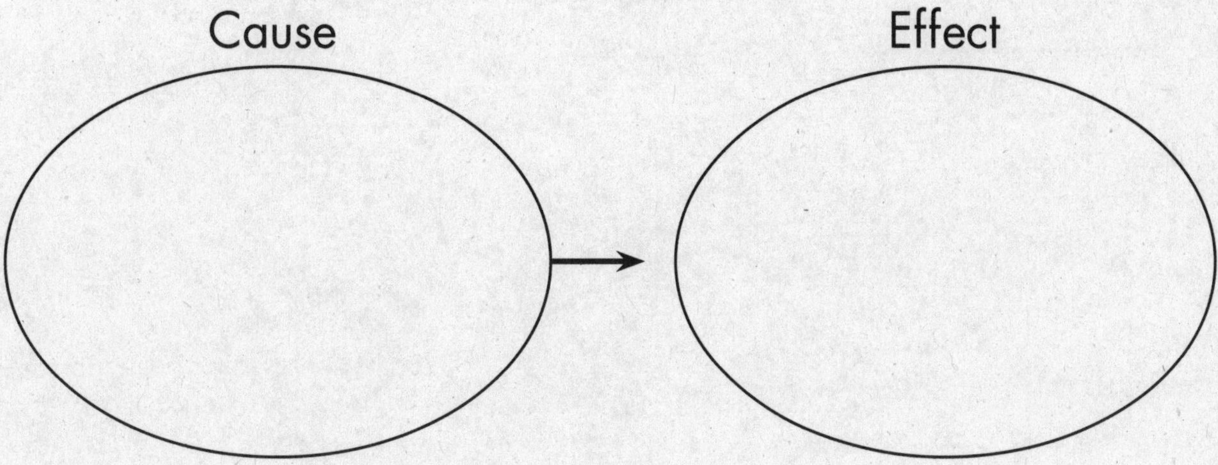

Directions: As you look at the pictures and read the paragraph, think about causes (why things happen) and effects (what things happen). Then answer the questions.
Home Activity: Your child learned about causes and effects. Flip a light switch. Turn a doorknob. State the effects: *The light comes on; the door opens.* Ask your child to state the cause of each effect.

Notes

Name ______________________________

Use with pages 71–73.

What do plants and animals need?

Before You Read Lesson 1

Read each sentence. Do you think it is true? Do you think it is not true? Circle the word or words after each sentence that tell what you think.

1. Most green plants are consumers. True Not True
2. Consumers cannot make their own food. True Not True
3. Large animals need more food than small animals. True Not True

After You Read Lesson 1

Read each sentence again. Circle the word or words after each sentence that tell what you think now. Did you change any answers? Put an **X** by each answer that you changed.

1. Most green plants are consumers. True Not True
2. Consumers cannot make their own food. True Not True
3. Large animals need more food than small animals. True Not True

Home Activity: Together talk about your child's answers. Have your child explain why his or her answers may have changed after reading the lesson.

Name ______________________

Use with pages 71–73.

Complete the Sentence

Write the word that completes each sentence.

producers	consumers	habitat	needs

1. Air, water, sunlight, and space to grow are ____________.

2. Plants are ____________, or living things that make their own food.

3. Animals are ____________, or living things that cannot make their own food.

4. The place where plants and animals live is their ____________.

Infer

5. Label each living thing as a producer or a consumer.

____________	____________
____________	____________

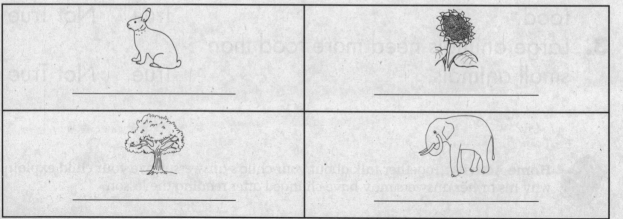

Name ______________________

Use with pages 74–77.

How do plants and animals get food in a grassland?

Before You Read Lesson 2

Read each sentence. Do you think it is true? Do you think it is not true? Circle the word or words after each sentence that tell what you think.

1.	All food chains start with the Sun.	True	Not True
2.	All food chains have predators and prey.	True	Not True
3.	Predators are animals that are caught and eaten.	True	Not True

After You Read Lesson 2

Read each sentence again. Circle the word or words after each sentence that tell what you think now. Did you change any answers? Put an **X** by each answer that you changed.

1.	All food chains start with the Sun.	True	Not True
2.	All food chains have predators and prey.	True	Not True
3.	Predators are animals that are caught and eaten.	True	Not True

Home Activity: Together talk about your child's answers. Have your child explain why his or her answers may have changed after reading the lesson.

Name ________________________________

Lesson 2 Review

Use with pages 74–77.

Complete the Sentence

Write the word or phrase that completes each sentence.

predator	prey	food web	food chain

1. A ______________ is the way energy gets from a plant to an animal.

2. An animal that catches and eats another animal is a ______________.

3. An animal that is caught and eaten is ______________.

4. A ______________ is all the ways energy gets from plants to animals in a habitat.

Cause and Effect

5. A worm saw a bird fly by. Birds eat worms, so the worm went into the soil to hide. Draw what caused the worm to go into the soil.

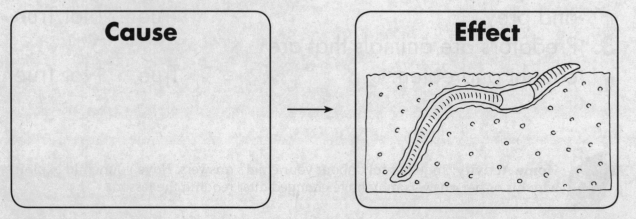

Cause	→	Effect

Name ______________________

Use with pages 78–81.

How do plants and animals get food in an ocean?

Before You Read Lesson 3

Read each sentence. Do you think it is true? Do you think it is not true? Circle the word or words after each sentence that tell what you think.

1. Plants are not part of the food chains in an ocean. True Not True
2. Energy passes through each step in a food chain. True Not True
3. A sea otter can get energy from the Sun. True Not True

After You Read Lesson 3

Read each sentence again. Circle the word or words after each sentence that tell what you think now. Did you change any answers? Put an **X** by each answer that you changed.

1. Plants are not part of the food chains in an ocean. True Not True
2. Energy passes through each step in a food chain. True Not True
3. A sea otter can get energy from the Sun. True Not True

Home Activity: Together talk about your child's answers. Have your child explain why his or her answers may have changed after reading the lesson.

Name ______________________________

Lesson 3 Review

Use with pages 78–81.

Complete the Sentence

Write the word or phrase that completes each sentence.

sunlight	kelp	energy	sea star

1. Animals eat plants to get ______________ to help them live and grow.

2. A sea urchin can eat ______________ for energy.

3. A sea otter can get energy from a ______________.

4. Energy passes from ______________ to kelp in an ocean food web.

Put Things in Order

5. Number the pictures 1–4 to show the order of this food chain.

Name ____________________

Use with pages 82–83.

What can cause a food web to change?

Before You Read Lesson 4

Read each sentence. Do you think it is true? Do you think it is not true? Circle the word or words after each sentence that tell what you think.

1. Animals and plants may die if a food chain changes. True Not True
2. People do not cause changes in a food chain. True Not True
3. An oil spill can cause changes in a food chain. True Not True

After You Read Lesson 4

Read each sentence again. Circle the word or words after each sentence that tell what you think now. Did you change any answers? Put an **X** by each answer that you changed.

1. Animals and plants may die if a food chain changes. True Not True
2. People do not cause changes in a food chain. True Not True
3. An oil spill can cause changes in a food chain. True Not True

Home Activity: Together talk about your child's answers. Have your child explain why his or her answers may have changed after reading the lesson.

Name ______________________________

Use with pages 82–83.

Complete the Sentence

Write the word that completes each sentence.

spill	accident	harm	web

1. Some changes in a food ______________ are caused by people.

2. Sometimes people do things that hurt, or ______________, animals.

3. Something that happens by mistake is an ______________.

4. When a ship carrying oil crashed, it caused an oil ______________.

Cause and Effect

5. Draw pictures that show the cause and the effect of an oil spill.

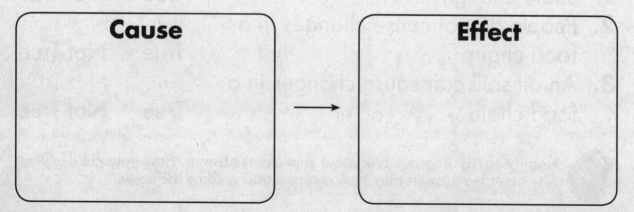

Cause → **Effect**

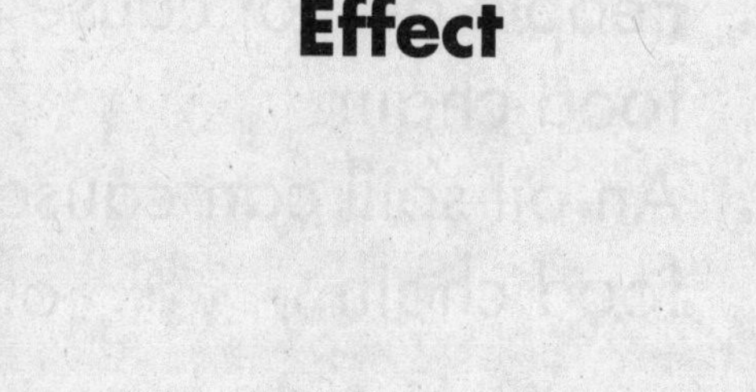

Name ______________________________

Use with pages 84–89.

How do plants and animals help each other?

Before You Read Lesson 5

Read each sentence. Do you think it is true? Do you think it is not true? Circle the word or words after each sentence that tell what you think.

1. Animals can help plants. True Not True
2. Some animals get help from other animals. True Not True
3. Squirrels use parts of plants to build nests. True Not True
4. Sharks do not help other animals. True Not True

After You Read Lesson 5

Read each sentence again. Circle the word or words after each sentence that tell what you think now. Did you change any answers? Put an **X** by each answer that you changed.

1. Animals can help plants. True Not True
2. Some animals get help from other animals. True Not True
3. Squirrels use parts of plants to build nests. True Not True
4. Sharks do not help other animals. True Not True

Home Activity: Together talk about your child's answers. Have your child explain why his or her answers may have changed after reading the lesson.

Name ______________________________

Lesson 5 Review

Use with pages 84–89.

Complete the Sentence

Write the word that completes each sentence.

shelter	nests	protect	reasons

1. Some animals get ____________ from plants.

2. Sea urchins ____________ cardinal fish.

3. Some animals use parts of plants to build ____________.

4. Animals need each other for many ____________.

Alike and Different

5. Write two ways that a shark and a crab are alike and two ways they are different.

Alike	Different

Name ______________________

Use with Chapter 3.

Comparing Lengths

These animals are all predators in ocean food webs. Read the table. Find out how long these animals can grow to be.

Animal	Length in m
Sea otter	1
Orca	9
Gray whale	13
Marlin	3
Blue shark	4

1. Which animal is the longest? ______________
2. Which animal is the shortest? ______________
3. How much longer is the orca than the blue shark? ______
4. Put the animals in order from longest to shortest.

____

____

____

____

____

Directions: Use the information in the table to answer the questions about the animals' lengths. Use what you know about ordering numbers to help you.
Home Activity: Your child learned how to use a table to compare data. Together measure the lengths of several kitchen utensils. Make a table showing the measurements in order from shortest to longest.

Notes

Family Science Activity

Make a Food Chain

Materials:
- paper
- crayons
- scissors
- glue

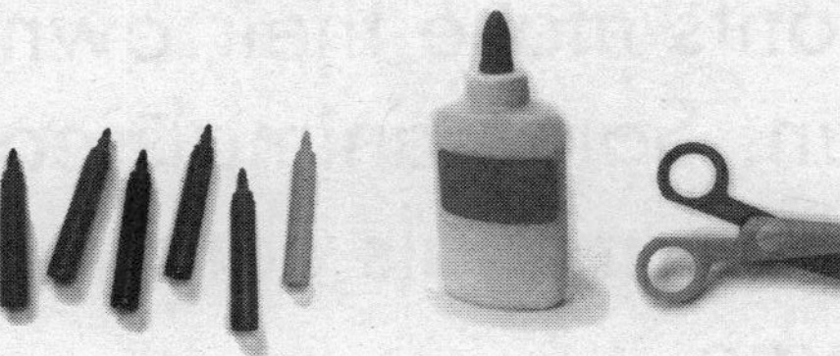

1. Talk about the food chain activity your child completed on page 3. Discuss food chains and how energy passes along a food chain. Explain that you are going to make a model of a food chain.
2. Cut a sheet of paper into 4 strips of equal size.
3. Ask your child to draw one thing from the food chain on each strip: the Sun, grass, a rabbit, and a fox.
4. Encourage your child to lay the strips in the order of the food chain.
5. Help your child make a paper chain. Put glue on one side of the first strip (with the Sun), then bring the other side around to form a loop. Glue the two ends together.
6. Continue with the next step in the food chain (grass). Put one end of this strip through the Sun link, then form a loop and glue it together.
7. Finish the chain by adding the remaining links. Display the finished paper food chain in a central area.

Take Home Booklet

Use with Chapter 3.

Dear Family,

Your child is learning about how plants and animals get what they need. In the science chapter How Plants and Animals Live Together, the class learned about food chains and food webs. The children also learned many ways that animals depend on plants and other animals for food, protection, and a place to live.

In addition to learning how changes in a food web can affect plants and animals, the children also learned many new vocabulary words. Help your child to make these words a part of his or her own vocabulary by using them when you talk together about animals.

producer
consumer
food chain
predator
prey
food web

The following pages include activities that you and your child can do together. By participating in your child's education, you will help to bring the learning home.

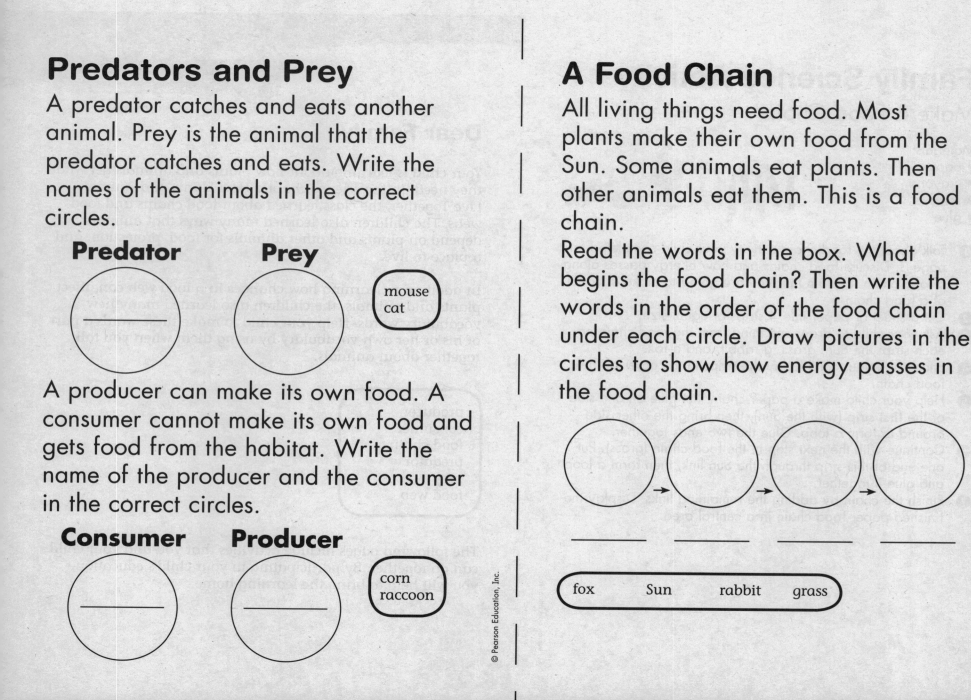

Predators and Prey

A predator catches and eats another animal. Prey is the animal that the predator catches and eats. Write the names of the animals in the correct circles.

Predator **Prey**

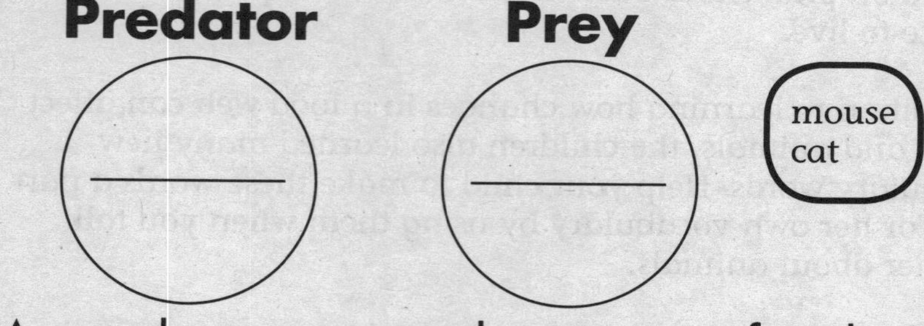

mouse
cat

A producer can make its own food. A consumer cannot make its own food and gets food from the habitat. Write the name of the producer and the consumer in the correct circles.

Consumer **Producer**

corn
raccoon

A Food Chain

All living things need food. Most plants make their own food from the Sun. Some animals eat plants. Then other animals eat them. This is a food chain.

Read the words in the box. What begins the food chain? Then write the words in the order of the food chain under each circle. Draw pictures in the circles to show how energy passes in the food chain.

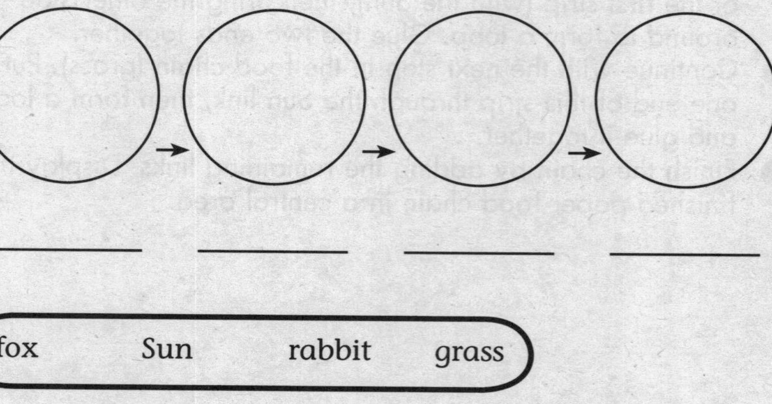

fox Sun rabbit grass

Name ______________________________

Use with Chapter 4.

Draw a picture or write a sentence to go with each word.

life cycle	nymph
seed coat	germinate
seedling	

Directions: Read the words and draw pictures to illustrate them or write sentences about them. Cut out the boxes to use as word cards.
Home Activity: Have your child use a picture in the chapter to explain the steps in the life cycle of an organism. Then have him or her tell how the terms *nymph, seed coat, germinate,* and *seedling* fit into different life cycles of organisms.

Name ______________________________

Use with Chapter 4.

Infer

Science Article

Maria planted flower seeds. Little plants soon came up. She watered them, and they grew. The plants made flowers. Later, Maria saw seeds where the flowers had been.

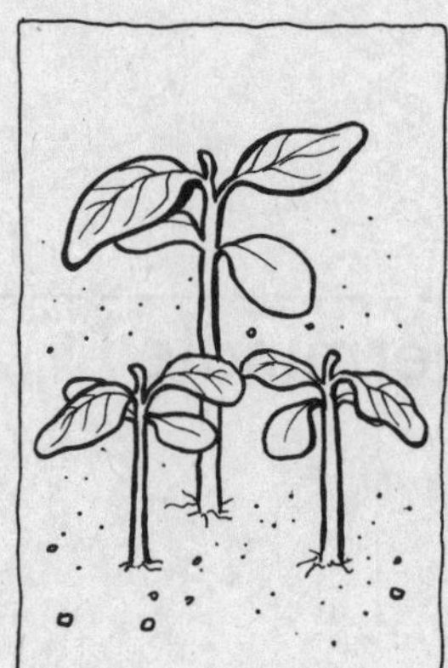

Apply It!

Infer What will happen next in this plant life cycle? Fill in the chart on the next page.

Name ______________________________

Use with Chapter 4.

I know	→	I can infer

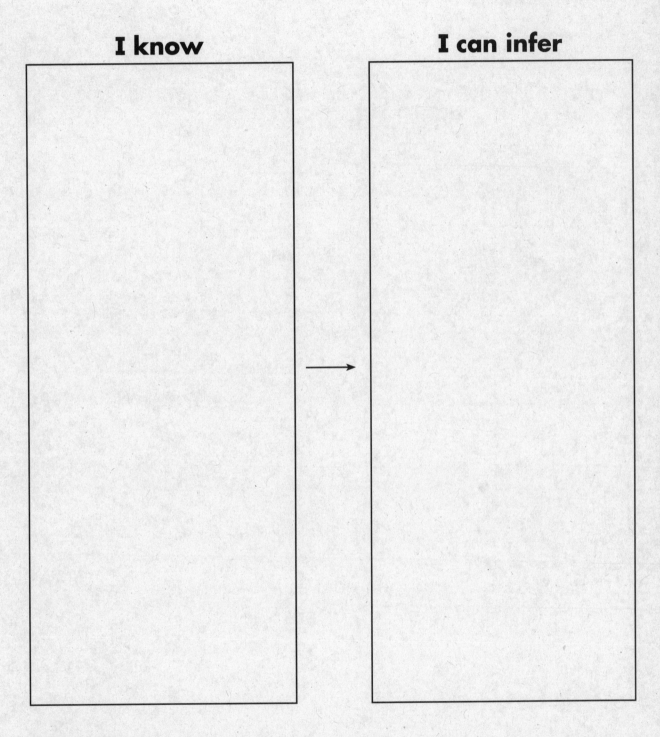

Directions: Read the Science Article on page 42. Write what you know in the *I know* box. Then write the answer to the question in the *I can infer* box.

Home Activity: Your child learned about making inferences. Find a newspaper or magazine article with pictures for you and your child to read together. Ask a question that requires your child to think about what he or she knows before answering.

Notes

Name ______________________________

Use with pages 103–107.

How do sea turtles grow and change?

Before You Read Lesson 1

Read each sentence. Do you think it is true? Do you think it is not true? Circle the word or words after each sentence that tell what you think.

1.	All living things grow and change.	True	Not True
2.	Sea turtles lay eggs in the sand.	True	Not True
3.	Baby turtles have a tooth.	True	Not True
4.	Baby turtles do not look like their parents.	True	Not True

After You Read Lesson 1

Read each sentence again. Circle the word or words after each sentence that tell what you think now. Did you change any answers? Put an **X** by each answer that you changed.

1.	All living things grow and change.	True	Not True
2.	Sea turtles lay eggs in the sand.	True	Not True
3.	Baby turtles have a tooth.	True	Not True
4.	Baby turtles do not look like their parents.	True	Not True

Home Activity: Together talk about your child's answers. Have your child explain why his or her answers may have changed after reading the lesson.

Name ______________________________

Lesson 1 Review

Use with pages 103–107.

Complete the Sentence

Write the word or phrase that completes each sentence.

live cycle	sea turtle	living thing	tooth

1. A plant or animal that grows and changes is a ______________.

2. A reptile that lives in the ocean and lays eggs on the beach is a ______________.

3. A body part that helps some baby animals break out of their egg is a ______________.

4. The way a living thing grows and changes is called its ______________.

Infer

5. A reptile lays an egg. Color the picture of an animal that could come from the egg.

Name ______________________________

Use with pages 108–109.

What is the life cycle of a dragonfly?

Before You Read Lesson 2

Read each sentence. Do you think it is true? Do you think it is not true? Circle the word or words after each sentence that tell what you think.

1.	Nymphs do not need wings.	True	Not True
2.	Nymphs shed their outside cover once.	True	Not True
3.	Dragonfly nymphs live in water.	True	Not True

After You Read Lesson 2

Read each sentence again. Circle the word or words after each sentence that tell what you think now. Did you change any answers? Put an **X** by each answer that you changed.

1.	Nymphs do not need wings.	True	Not True
2.	Nymphs shed their outside cover once.	True	Not True
3.	Dragonfly nymphs live in water.	True	Not True

Home Activity: Together talk about your child's answers. Have your child explain why his or her answers may have changed after reading the lesson.

Name ______________________________

Use with pages 108–111.

Complete the Sentence

Write the word that completes each sentence.

dragonfly	nymph	water	eggs

1. Insects are born in ____________ and then crawl to land.

2. Insects hatch from ____________.

3. A ____________ is a young bug without wings that sheds its covering many times.

4. A ____________ is an adult bug with wings that can lay eggs.

Infer

5. Is this a picture of a nymph or an adult cicada? How do you know?

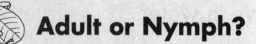

Adult or Nymph?

____

____

Name ______________________

Use with pages 110–111.

What is the life cycle of a horse?

Before You Read Lesson 3

Read each sentence. Do you think it is true? Do you think it is not true? Circle the word or words after each sentence that tell what you think.

1.	A baby horse is called a mammal.	True	Not True
2.	A foal drinks milk from its mother.	True	Not True
3.	A foal looks like its parents.	True	Not True

After You Read Lesson 3

Read each sentence again. Circle the word or words after each sentence that tell what you think now. Did you change any answers? Put an **X** by each answer that you changed.

1.	A baby horse is called a mammal.	True	Not True
2.	A foal drinks milk from its mother.	True	Not True
3.	A foal looks like its parents.	True	Not True

Home Activity: Together talk about your child's answers. Have your child explain why his or her answers may have changed after reading the lesson.

Complete the Sentence

Write the word that completes each sentence.

foal	mothers	horses	parents

1. Your mom and dad are also called your ______________.

2. Mammals grow inside their ______________.

3. A young horse is a ______________.

4. Young ______________ look like their parents.

Put Things in Order

5. How does an egg turn into an adult bird? Number the pictures 1–3 to show the life cycle of a bird.

Name ______________________________

Use with pages 112–113.

How are young animals like their parents?

Before You Read Lesson 4

Read each sentence. Do you think it is true? Do you think it is not true? Circle the word or words after each sentence that tell what you think.

1. Baby penguins have fuzzy feathers. True Not True

2. Most animal parents and babies have the same shape. True Not True

3. The spots of young and adult giraffes look the same. True Not True

After You Read Lesson 4

Read each sentence again. Circle the word or words after each sentence that tell what you think now. Did you change any answers? Put an **X** by each answer that you changed.

1. Baby penguins have fuzzy feathers. True Not True

2. Most animal parents and babies have the same shape. True Not True

3. The spots of young and adult giraffes look the same. True Not True

Home Activity: Together talk about your child's answers. Have your child explain why his or her answers may have changed after reading the lesson.

Name ______________________________

Lesson 4 Review

Use with pages 112–113.

Complete the Sentence

Write the word that completes each sentence.

pattern	same	shape	different

1. Young animals often look like their parents in ______________ and color.

2. Some young animals look ______________ from their parents.

3. Each giraffe has its own ______________ of spots.

4. No two patterns are the ______________.

Infer

5. How are young animals like their parents? Complete the chart by drawing a baby giraffe.

Baby Animal	Adult Animal

Name ______________________________

Use with pages 114–115.

What is the life cycle of a bean plant?

Before You Read Lesson 5

Read each sentence. Do you think it is true? Do you think it is not true? Circle the word or words after each sentence that tell what you think.

1.	A seedling may germinate.	True	Not True
2.	A tiny plant is inside a seed.	True	Not True
3.	Adult plant flowers make seeds.	True	Not True

After You Read Lesson 5

Read each sentence again. Circle the word or words after each sentence that tell what you think now. Did you change any answers? Put an **X** by each answer that you changed.

1.	A seedling may germinate.	True	Not True
2.	A tiny plant is inside a seed.	True	Not True
3.	Adult plant flowers make seeds.	True	Not True

Home Activity: Together talk about your child's answers. Have your child explain why his or her answers may have changed after reading the lesson.

Name ______________________________

Lesson 5 Review

Use with pages 114–115.

Complete the Sentence

Write the word or phrase that completes each sentence.

seed coat	seedling	germinate	seeds

1. A ______________ is a hard outer covering of a seed.

2. A seed that gets water and air may ______________, or grow into a new plant.

3. A ______________ is a young plant.

4. The flowers on an adult plant make ______________.

Put Things in Order

5. How does a plant grow? Complete the life cycle for this seedling by drawing seeds and an adult plant.

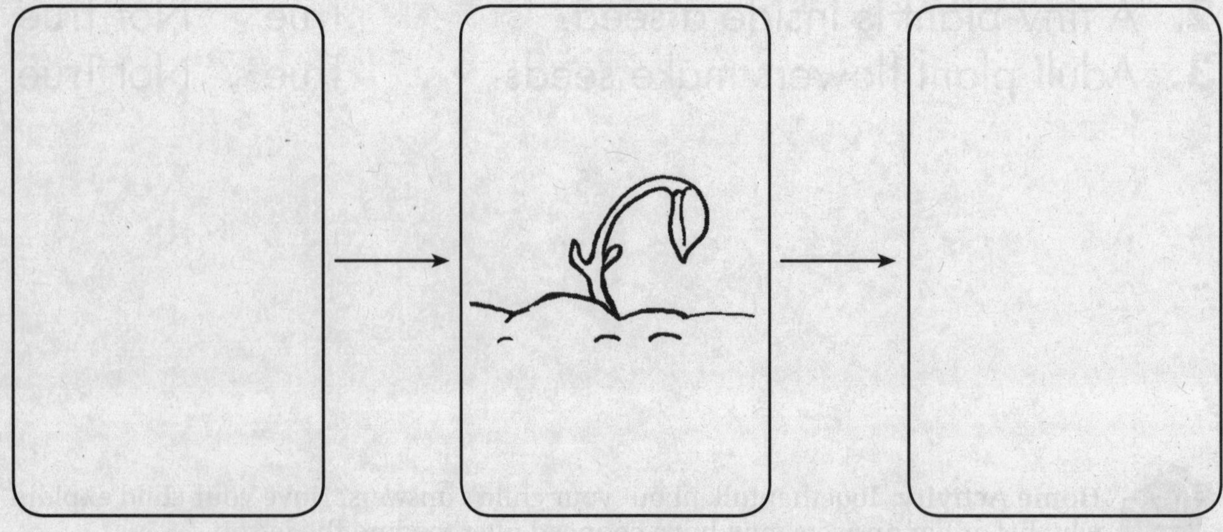

Name ______________________

Use with pages 116–117.

How are young plants like their parents?

Before You Read Lesson 6

Read each sentence. Do you think it is true? Do you think it is not true? Circle the word or words after each sentence that tell what you think.

1. Parent plants and their young usually look alike. True Not True
2. A young saguaro cactus grows arms. True Not True
3. Some young plants have flowers with different colors than their parents. True Not True

After You Read Lesson 6

Read each sentence again. Circle the word or words after each sentence that tell what you think now. Did you change any answers? Put an **X** by each answer that you changed.

1. Parent plants and their young usually look alike. True Not True
2. A young saguaro cactus grows arms. True Not True
3. Some young plants have flowers with different colors than their parents. True Not True

Home Activity: Together talk about your child's answers. Have your child explain why his or her answers may have changed after reading the lesson.

Name ______________________________

Use with pages 116–117.

Complete the Sentence

Write the word that completes each sentence.

color	foxglove	saguaro	up

1. Young plants can be like their parents in __________.

2. A young saguaro cactus grows straight __________ from the ground.

3. A __________ cactus does not grow arms until it is 65 years old.

4. A __________ is a flower that does not grow flowers until it is two years old.

Alike and Different

5. Write one way that a young cactus and its parent plant are alike and one way they are different.

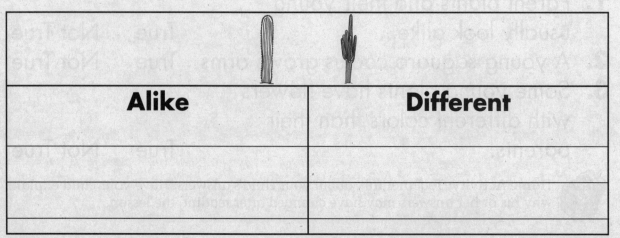

Alike	Different

Name ____________________

Use with pages 118–121.

How do people grow and change?

Before You Read Lesson 7

Read each sentence. Do you think it is true? Do you think it is not true? Circle the word or words after each sentence that tell what you think.

1. To change, people must grow. True Not True
2. People differ in height and eye and hair color. True Not True
3. Children in one family can look different. True Not True

After You Read Lesson 7

Read each sentence again. Circle the word or words after each sentence that tell what you think now. Did you change any answers? Put an **X** by each answer that you changed.

1. To change, people must grow. True Not True
2. People differ in height and eye and hair color. True Not True
3. Children in one family can look different. True Not True

Home Activity: Together talk about your child's answers. Have your child explain why his or her answers may have changed after reading the lesson.

Name ______________________

Use with pages 118–121.

Complete the Sentence

Write the word that completes each sentence.

grow	babies	teenagers	adult

1. People are ____________ when they are born.

2. As young children grow older, they become ____________.

3. An ____________ keeps changing but does not grow taller.

4. All people change as they ____________.

Infer

5. Draw a picture of how you look now. Then draw a picture of how you might look as an adult.

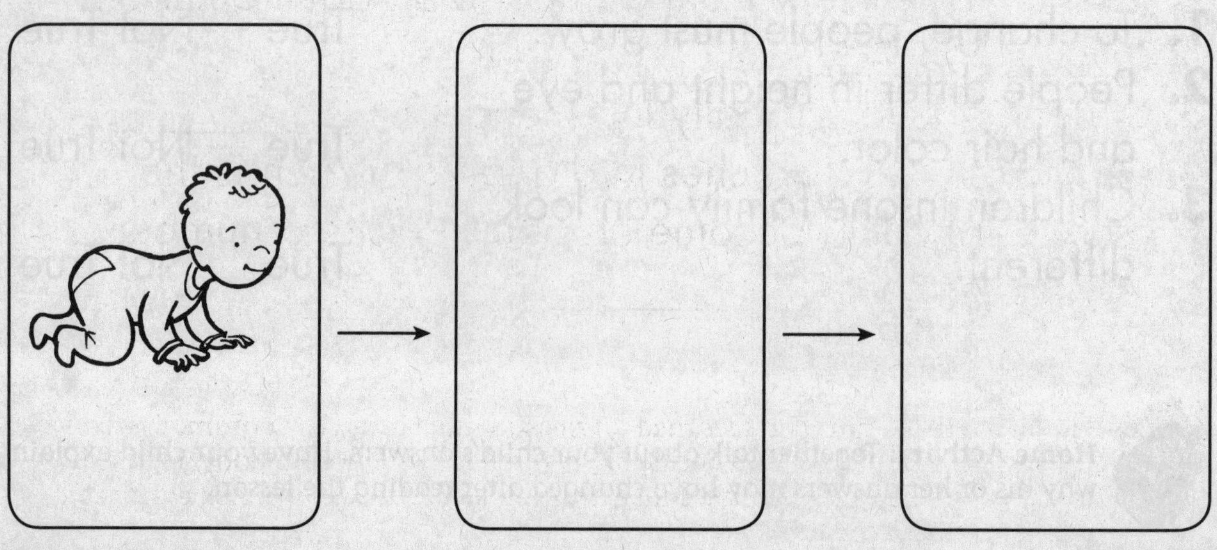

Name ______________________________

Use with Chapter 4.

Measuring Time

The table compares the life cycles of two kinds of flies.

Life Cycles of Housefly and Greenhouse Whitefly Compared		
Stage	**Housefly**	**Greenhouse Whitefly**
Egg	1 day	9 days
Larva	5 to 14 days	30 to 35 days
Pupa	3 to 10 days	11 days
Adult	19 to 70 days	10 to 40 days

Directions: Use the information in the table to answer the questions.

1. How many days does it take a greenhouse whitefly egg to hatch into a larva? ____________
2. Which fly hatches from a pupa to an adult quicker? ______________
3. Which adult fly usually lives longer? ____________
4. A housefly egg hatches into a larva. When is the soonest it could become an adult? Write a number sentence. _________________

Home Activity: Your child learned to measure time using a diagram. Discuss the life cycle for people and decide on average time spent as a baby, toddler, child, young adult, and adult. Make a table like the one above. Ask each other questions about the table.

Notes

Family Science Activity

How People Grow and Change

Materials:

- Drawing paper
- Old magazines
- Scissors
- Glue
- Pen or pencil

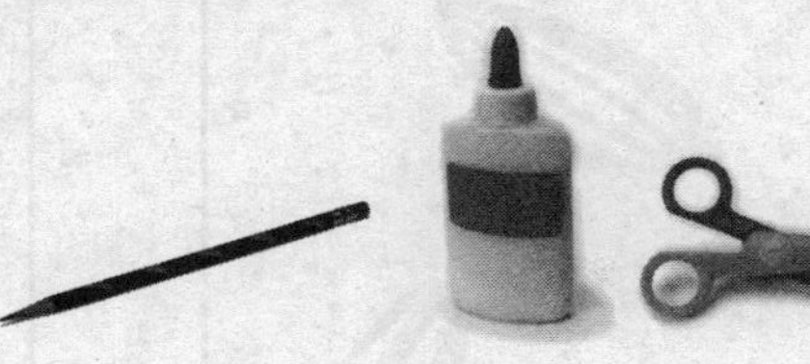

Steps

1. Talk with your child about how people change as they grow. Discuss what a baby is like. Ask your child to talk about how he or she has changed. Discuss different ways that adults change as they grow.
2. Write the following labels from left to right on a large sheet of paper, or each one on a separate sheet of paper: **Baby, Child, Teenager, Adult**.
3. Help your child cut out images of babies, children, teenagers, and adults of different ages in the magazines.
4. Glue the images in groups under the appropriate labels.
5. Help your child write a few sentences under each group of images to describe what people in that age group are like. You might mention what people in that group can and cannot do. You can also compare people in that age group with people in the previous or following age group.
6. Encourage your child to show the collages to a friend or family member and to discuss how people change as they grow.

Take Home Booklet

Use with Chapter 4.

Dear Family,

Your child is learning about how living things grow in different ways. In the science chapter How Living Things Grow and Change, our class has learned about the life cycles of various animals and plants. The children have also learned ways in which people grow and change.

In addition to learning how living things are like and different from their parents, the children have also learned many new vocabulary words. Help your child to make these words a part of his or her own vocabulary by using them when you talk together about animals.

life cycle
nymph
seed coat
germinate
seedling

These following pages include activities that you and your child can do together. By participating in your child's education, you will help to bring the learning home.

The Life Cycle of a Sunflower

Look at the four pictures that show the life cycle of a sunflower. Use words from the word bank to write a sentence that tells about each picture. Then color in the pictures.

seed
germinate
seedling
flower

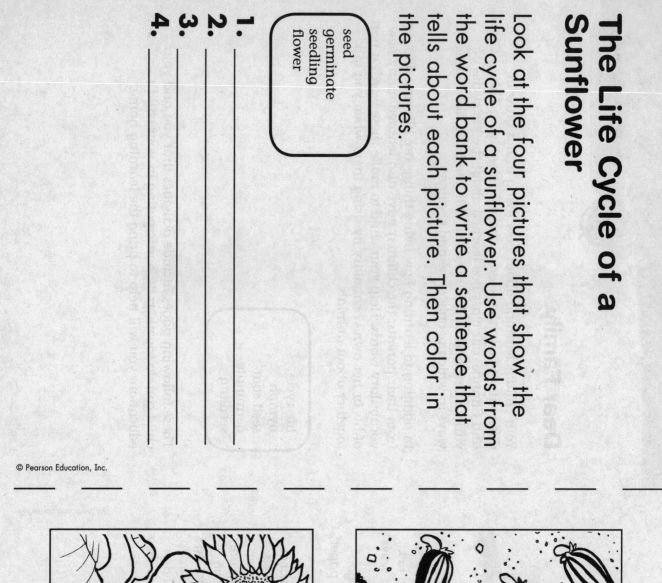

1. ______________________
2. ______________________
3. ______________________
4. ______________________

1

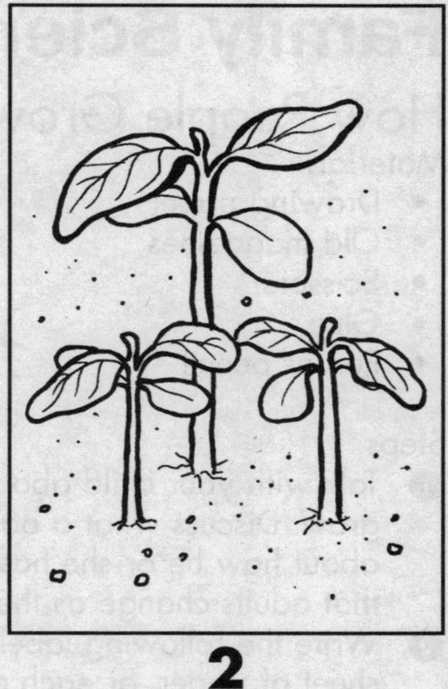

2

3

4

Name ______________________________

Vocabulary Preview

Use with Chapter 5.

Draw a picture or write a sentence to go with each word.

boulder	erosion
weathering	natural resource
sand	pollution
minerals	recycle

Directions: Read the words and draw pictures to illustrate them or write sentences about them. Cut out the boxes to use as word cards.
Home Activity: Give clues to the vocabulary words, such as *Old cans made into new cans* and *Dirty air, land, or water,* and have your child say the correct words.

Name ________________________________

Use with Chapter 5.

Picture Clues

Read the science article.

Collect and Recycle

People can help keep Earth clean. One way is to collect newspaper, metal cans, and plastic bottles. These things can be recycled, or changed and used again.

Name ______________________

Use with Chapter 5.

Apply It!

Observe What things can people collect and recycle? Look for clues in the picture on page 56. Fill in the chart.

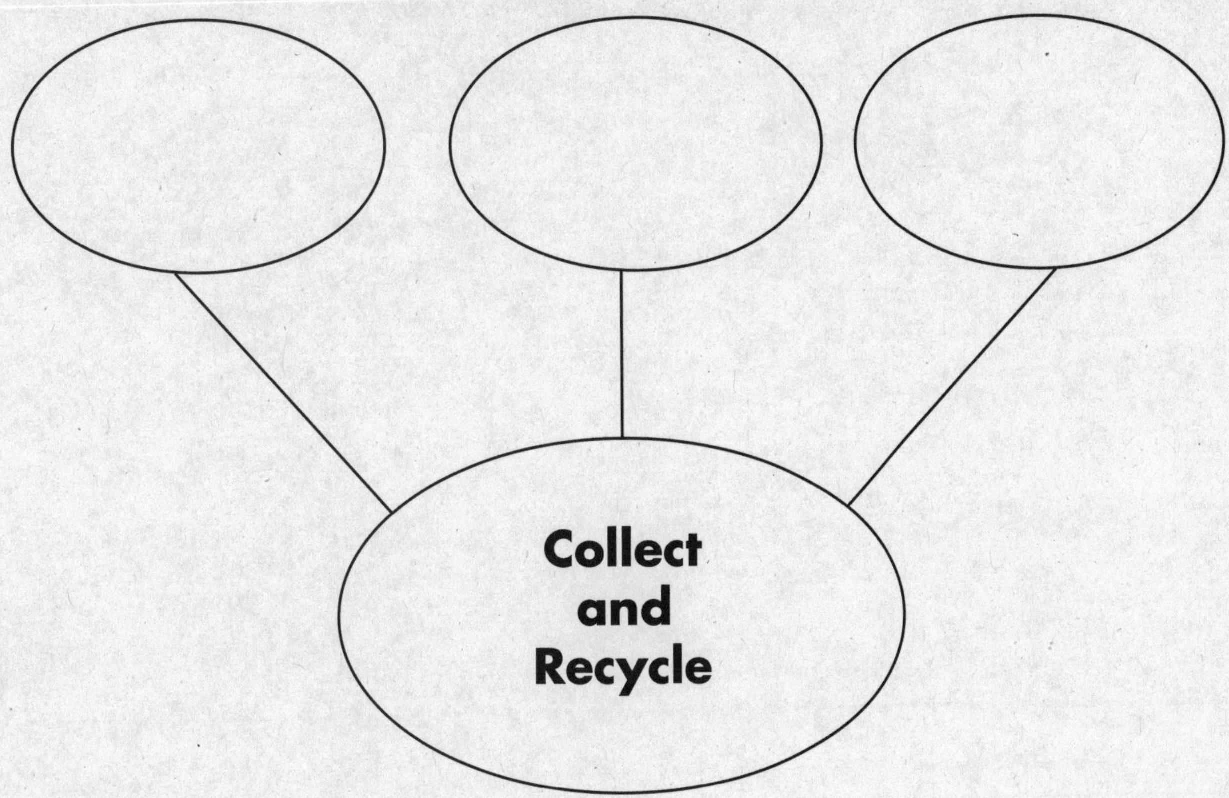

Directions: Read the Science Article and look at the picture. Then answer the question by filling in the chart.
Home Activity: Your child learned about picture clues. Look for a picture in a newspaper or magazine. Cover the caption and discuss with your child what he or she thinks the picture is about. Then read the caption and discuss.

Notes

Name ______________________________

Use with pages 143–145.

What are natural resources?

Before You Read Lesson 1

Read each sentence. Do you think it is true? Do you think it is not true? Circle the word or words after each sentence that tell what you think.

1.	Sunlight is a natural resource.	True	Not True
2.	Oil is a natural resource that can be replaced.	True	Not True
3.	Water and air will never be used up.	True	Not True

After You Read Lesson 1

Read each sentence again. Circle the word or words after each sentence that tell what you think now. Did you change any answers? Put an **X** by each answer that you changed.

1.	Sunlight is a natural resource.	True	Not True
2.	Oil is a natural resource that can be replaced.	True	Not True
3.	Water and air will never be used up.	True	Not True

Home Activity: Together talk about your child's answers. Have your child explain why his or her answers may have changed after reading the lesson.

Name ______________________

Lesson 1 Review

Use with pages 143–145.

Complete the Sentence

Write the word or phrase that completes each sentence.

wind	fresh water	salt water	natural resource

1. Something useful that comes from Earth is a __________.

2. The water in ponds, rivers, streams, and lakes is __________.

3. The water in oceans is __________.

4. Air that moves is __________.

Predict

5. Draw two ways you will use water today.

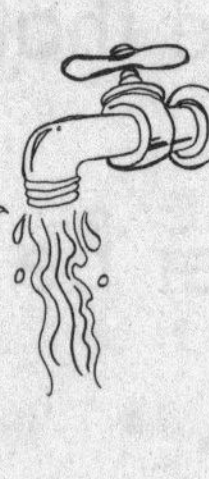

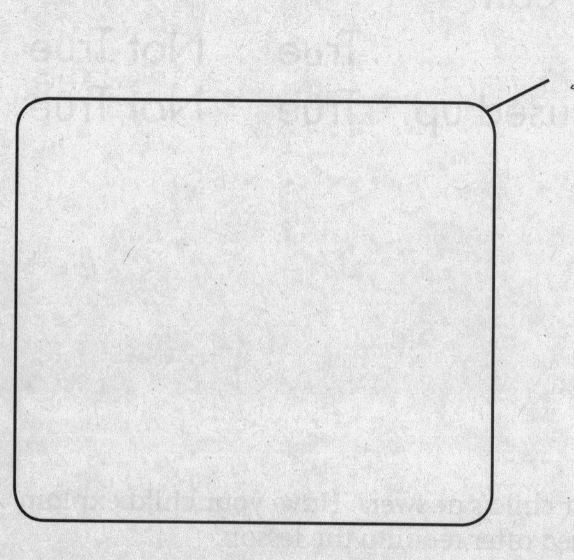

Name ______________________

Use with pages 146–149.

What are rocks and soil like?

Before You Read Lesson 2

Read each sentence. Do you think it is true? Do you think it is not true? Circle the word or words after each sentence that tell what you think.

1.	A boulder is a small rock.	True	Not True
2.	Sand is made of tiny pieces of rock.	True	Not True
3.	Rocks are made of minerals.	True	Not True
4.	Soil is always dark, hard, and wet.	True	Not True

After You Read Lesson 2

Read each sentence again. Circle the word or words after each sentence that tell what you think now. Did you change any answers? Put an **X** by each answer that you changed.

1.	A boulder is a small rock.	True	Not True
2.	Sand is made of tiny pieces of rock.	True	Not True
3.	Rocks are made of minerals.	True	Not True
4.	Soil is always dark, hard, and wet.	True	Not True

Home Activity: Together talk about your child's answers. Have your child explain why his or her answers may have changed after reading the lesson.

Name ______________________________

Lesson 2 Review

Use with pages 146–149.

Complete the Sentence

Write the word that completes each sentence.

boulder	sand	minerals	soil

1. A ______________ is a very large rock.

2. Tiny pieces of rock make up ______________.

3. Gold, iron, and silver are ______________.

4. A natural resource that covers most of the land is ______________.

Picture Clues

5. Color anything in this picture that needs soil to grow.

Name ______________________________

Use with pages 150–151.

How do people use plants?

Before You Read Lesson 3

Read each sentence. Do you think it is true? Do you think it is not true? Circle the word or words after each sentence that tell what you think.

1. Plants can be used as food. True Not True
2. Plants cannot be used to make clothes. True Not True
3. A newspaper is made from plants. True Not True

After You Read Lesson 3

Read each sentence again. Circle the word or words after each sentence that tell what you think now. Did you change any answers? Put an **X** by each answer that you changed.

1. Plants can be used as food. True Not True
2. Plants cannot be used to make clothes. True Not True
3. A newspaper is made from plants. True Not True

Home Activity: Together talk about your child's answers. Have your child explain why his or her answers may have changed after reading the lesson.

Name ______________________________

Use with pages 150–151.

Complete the Sentence

Write the word or phrase that completes each sentence.

food	natural resource	wood	cotton

1. Plants are a ______________.
2. Plants can be used to make ______________, shelter, and clothing.
3. The natural resource used to make baseball bats is ______________.
4. People use ______________ to make some clothes.

Picture Clues

5. Things we use every day are made from natural resources. Match the picture with the natural resource it comes from.

trees wheat cotton water

______________	______________
______________	CEREAL RICE PASTA ______________

Name ______________________________

Use with pages 152–153.

How does Earth change?

Before You Read Lesson 4

Read each sentence. Do you think it is true? Do you think it is not true? Circle the word or words after each sentence that tell what you think.

1.	Erosion can change Earth.	True	Not True
2.	Plant roots can help stop erosion.	True	Not True
3.	Weathering is when rocks or soil are moved by water or wind.	True	Not True

After You Read Lesson 4

Read each sentence again. Circle the word or words after each sentence that tell what you think now. Did you change any answers? Put an **X** by each answer that you changed.

1.	Erosion can change Earth.	True	Not True
2.	Plant roots can help stop erosion.	True	Not True
3.	Weathering is when rocks or soil are moved by water or wind.	True	Not True

Home Activity: Together talk about your child's answers. Have your child explain why his or her answers may have changed after reading the lesson.

Name ______________________________

Lesson 4 Review

Use with pages 152–153.

Complete the Sentence

Write the word that completes each sentence.

Erosion	Weathering	Roots	Temperature

1. ______________ changes can cause weathering.
2. ______________ happens when water or wind move rocks and soil.
3. ______________ happens when rocks break apart and change.
4. ______________ of plants help hold soil in place.

Cause and Effect

5. What causes erosion? Color the thing in each picture that causes changes in soil or rock.

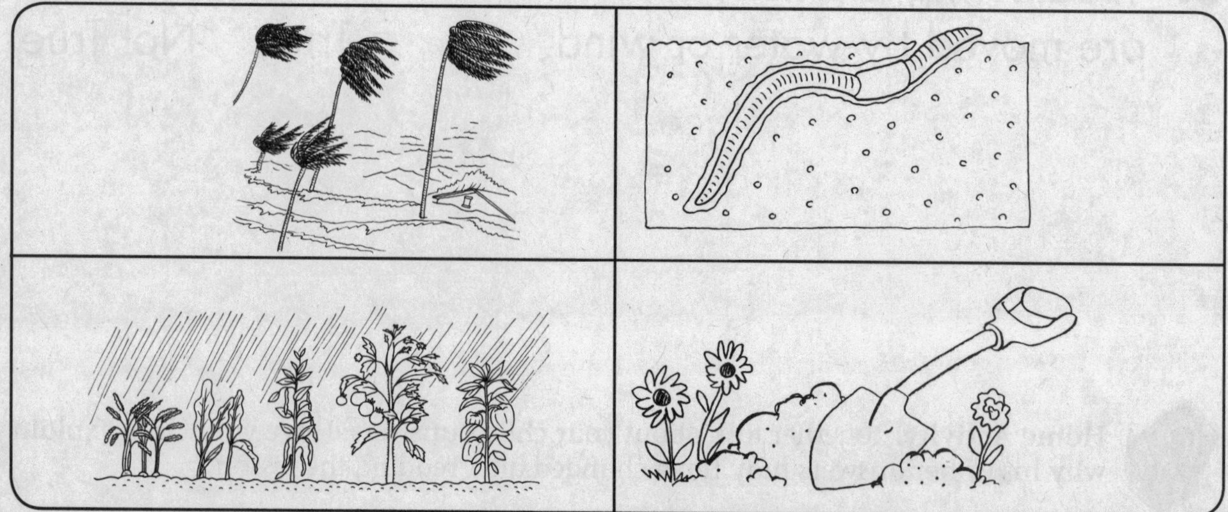

Name ____________________

Use with pages 154–159.

How can people help protect Earth?

Before You Read Lesson 5

Read each sentence. Do you think it is true? Do you think it is not true? Circle the word or words after each sentence that tell what you think.

1. People can help reduce pollution. True Not True
2. Paper and plastic can be recycled. True Not True
3. Trees cannot be replaced. True Not True
4. Plants and animals are safe in a refuge. True Not True

After You Read Lesson 5

Read each sentence again. Circle the word or words after each sentence that tell what you think now. Did you change any answers? Put an **X** by each answer that you changed.

1. People can help reduce pollution. True Not True
2. Paper and plastic can be recycled. True Not True
3. Trees cannot be replaced. True Not True
4. Plants and animals are safe in a refuge. True Not True

Home Activity: Together talk about your child's answers. Have your child explain why his or her answers may have changed after reading the lesson.

Name ______________________________

Lesson 5 Review

Use with pages 154–159.

Complete the Sentence

Write the word that completes each sentence.

pollution	recycle	litter	refuge

1. Something harmful that is added to the land, air, or water causes ____________.

2. Trash on the ground is ____________.

3. To change something so it can be used again is to ____________.

4. A ____________ is a safe place for plants and animals to live.

Picture Clues

5. Color a kind of pollution you see in the picture.

Name ________________________________

Bird Count

Mrs. Sung's second-grade class visited a bird refuge last week. The students counted the number of ducks, cranes, and geese they saw on a pond. They made a bar graph to show how many of each kind of bird they saw.

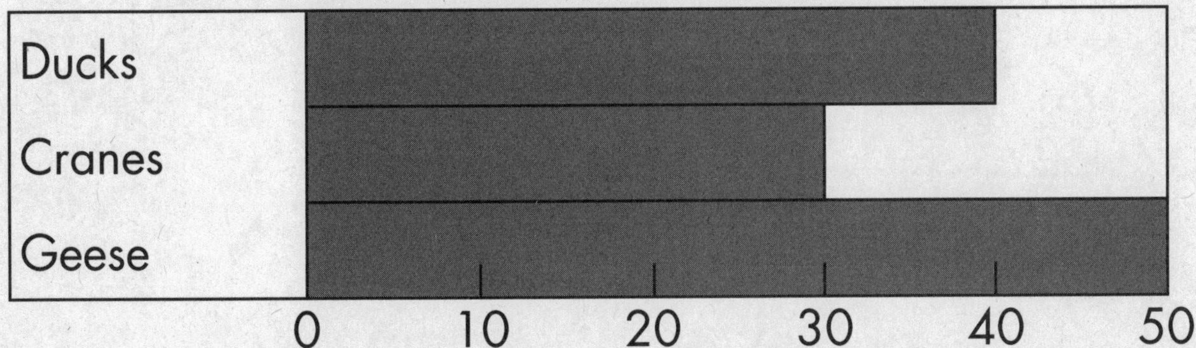

Use the bar graph to answer these questions.

1. How many ducks did the students see? __________
2. How many more geese than cranes did the students see? __________
3. Write a number sentence that shows how many ducks and cranes the students saw. ____________________

Directions: Look at the bar graph and note how many of each kind of bird the students saw. Then use those numbers to answer the questions.
Home Activity: Your child learned how to interpret a bar graph. Together count how many glasses, mugs, and dinner plates you have and make a bar graph like the one on this page. Then ask your child questions about the bar graph.

Notes

Family Science Activity

Natural Resources at Home

Materials:
- Lined paper or a notebook
- Pen or pencil

Steps
1. Talk with your child about the different natural resources that people use. Discuss how people use natural resources directly (for example, breathing air or drinking water) and indirectly (for example, using paper made from trees, wearing clothes made from cotton, or using machines that run on electricity that comes from burning coal or sunlight or wind).
2. Look around your home with your child. Write each natural resource that you use on a separate sheet of paper. On each sheet, record the different ways you use that resource in your home, directly and indirectly.
3. Look at your lists. Talk about how you can use less of, reuse, or recycle one of those resources.
4. Make a plan, and put it into action!

Take Home Booklet

Use with Chapter 5.

Dear Family,

Your child is learning about Earth's natural resources. In the science chapter Earth's Land, Air, and Water, our class has learned about each of these resources and some ways that people use them. The children have also learned about how Earth changes and what people can do to protect its resources.

In addition to learning how people need and use land, air, and water, the children have also learned many new vocabulary words. Help your child to make these words a part of his or her own vocabulary by using them when you talk together about land, air, and water.

natural resource
boulder
sand
minerals
weathering
erosion
pollution
recycle

These following pages include activities that you and your child can do together. By participating in your child's education, you will help to bring the learning home.

Draw a picture showing one way you can reuse a metal can. Tell about your picture.

Vocabulary Scramble

The letters of each word below are all mixed up. Look at each group of letters. Decide what vocabulary word the letters spell. Then, write the word on the line. If you need help, look at the vocabulary words in the box below.

NELIMARS __________

UDBELOR __________

SIONROE __________

ATRINGHEWE __________

LUTPIONOL __________

ECLERCY __________

boulder
erosion
mineral
pollution
recycle
weathering

Name ______________________

Use with Chapter 6.

Draw a picture or write a sentence to go with each word.

tornado	hurricane
water cycle	lightning
evaporate	migrate
condense	hibernate

Directions: Read the words and draw pictures to illustrate them or write sentences about them. Cut out the boxes to use as word cards.
Home Activity: Ask your child to explain the difference between a *tornado* and a *hurricane* and between animals that *migrate* and animals that *hibernate*. Have your child tell how *evaporate* and *condense* are related to the water cycle.

Name ______________________________

Use with Chapter 6.

Draw Conclusions

Look at the picture.

Science Picture

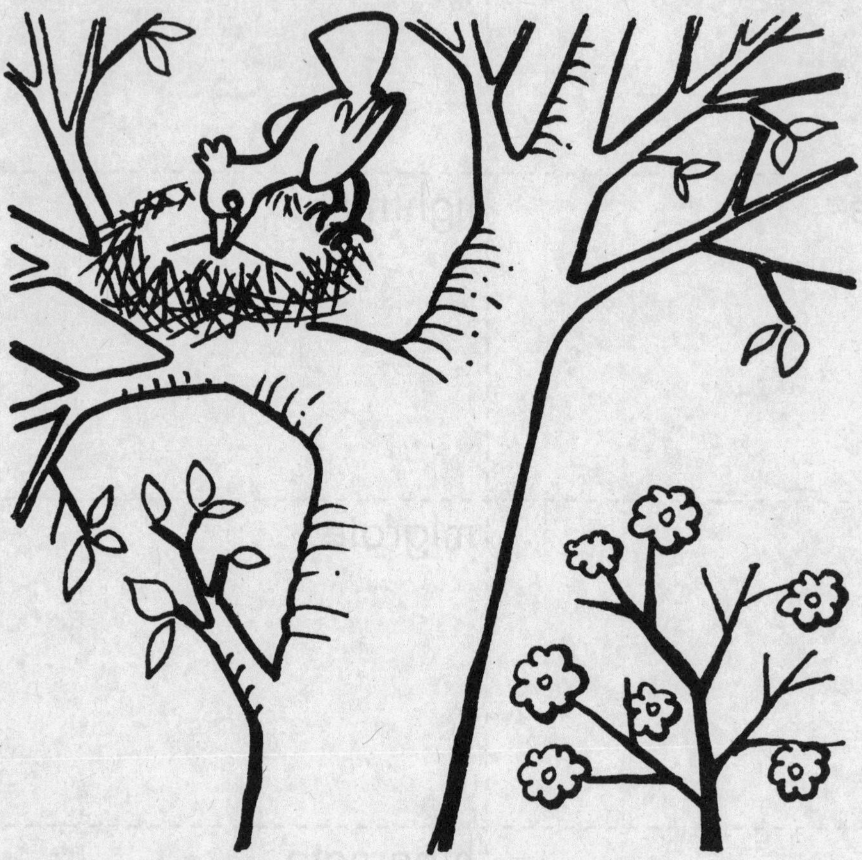

Name ______________________________

Use with Chapter 6.

Apply It!

Infer What season of the year is it? Fill in the chart.

I know	My conclusion

Directions: Look at the picture. Write what you see in the picture in the *I know* box. Use that information to draw a conclusion that answers the question. Write your conclusion in the *My Conclusion* box.

Home Activity: Your child learned about drawing conclusions. Find a newspaper or magazine picture that shows a scene. Cover the caption and ask your child to draw a conclusion about the picture. Encourage your child to offer reasons for the conclusion.

Notes

Name ___________________________

Use with pages 175–177.

What are some kinds of weather?

Before You Read Lesson 1

Read each sentence. Do you think it is true? Do you think it is not true? Circle the word or words after each sentence that tell what you think.

1.	Weather can be hot or cold and wet or dry.	True	Not True
2.	Sleet is one kind of wet weather.	True	Not True
3.	Snow falls when the air is very warm.	True	Not True

After You Read Lesson 1

Read each sentence again. Circle the word or words after each sentence that tell what you think now. Did you change any answers? Put an **X** by each answer that you changed.

1.	Weather can be hot or cold and wet or dry.	True	Not True
2.	Sleet is one kind of wet weather.	True	Not True
3.	Snow falls when the air is very warm.	True	Not True

Home Activity: Together talk about your child's answers. Have your child explain why his or her answers may have changed after reading the lesson.

Name ______________________________

Use with pages 175–177.

Complete the Sentence

Write the word that completes each sentence.

Weather	Sleet	Drought	Blizzards

1. ____________ is what the air outside is like.

2. ____________ are snowstorms with strong, cold winds.

3. ____________ is rain that freezes as it falls from clouds.

4. ____________ is when it does not rain for a long time.

Draw Conclusions

5. What is the weather like in this picture?

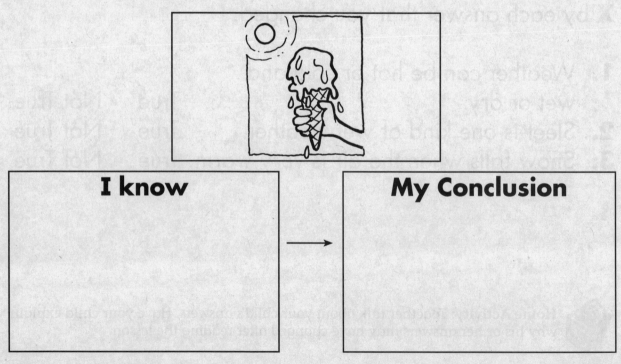

I know	→	My Conclusion

Name ______________________

Use with pages 178–179.

What is the water cycle?

Before You Read Lesson 2

Read each sentence. Do you think it is true? Do you think it is not true? Circle the word or words after each sentence that tell what you think.

1. Clouds are not part of the water cycle. True Not True

2. Some water changes into water vapor. True Not True

3. Water vapor condenses when it gets cold. True Not True

After You Read Lesson 2

Read each sentence again. Circle the word or words after each sentence that tell what you think now. Did you change any answers? Put an **X** by each answer that you changed.

1. Clouds are not part of the water cycle. True Not True

2. Some water changes into water vapor. True Not True

3. Water vapor condenses when it gets cold. True Not True

Home Activity: Together talk about your child's answers. Have your child explain why his or her answers may have changed after reading the lesson.

Name ______________________________

Lesson 2 Review

Use with pages 178–179.

Complete the Sentence

Write the word or phrase that completes each sentence.

condenses	evaporates	water vapor	water cycle

1. The way water moves between the clouds and Earth is the ______________.

2. When water vapor changes into tiny drops of water, it ______________.

3. When water changes into water vapor, it ____________.

4. Water in the air is ______________.

Draw Conclusions

5. How does water get from clouds to Earth?

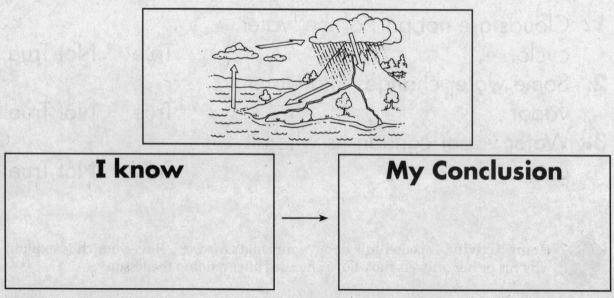

I know	→	My Conclusion

Name ______________________________

Use with pages 180–181.

What is spring?

Before You Read Lesson 3

Read each sentence. Do you think it is true? Do you think it is not true? Circle the word or words after each sentence that tell what you think.

1. Spring is one of the four seasons. True Not True
2. Spring days are very hot. True Not True
3. Many animals have babies. True Not True

After You Read Lesson 3

Read each sentence again. Circle the word or words after each sentence that tell what you think now. Did you change any answers? Put an **X** by each answer that you changed.

1. Spring is one of the four seasons. True Not True
2. Spring days are very hot. True Not True
3. Many animals have babies. True Not True

Home Activity: Together talk about your child's answers. Have your child explain why his or her answers may have changed after reading the lesson.

Name ______________________________

Use with pages 180–181.

Complete the Sentence

Write the word that completes each sentence.

babies	seasons	repeat	rains

1. The four ______________ are spring, summer, fall, and winter.

2. The seasons ______________ every year.

3. Many animals have ______________ in the spring.

4. Plants grow well in the spring because it usually ______________ a lot.

Infer

5. The weather can help us decide what to wear. Draw a picture of how you dress in spring.

Name ___________________________

Think, Read, Learn

Use with pages 182–183.

What is summer?

Before You Read Lesson 4

Read each sentence. Do you think it is true? Do you think it is not true? Circle the word or words after each sentence that tell what you think.

1.	Summer is cooler than spring.	True	Not True
2.	Summer has a lot of daylight hours.	True	Not True
3.	Many trees grow green leaves in summer.	True	Not True

After You Read Lesson 4

Read each sentence again. Circle the word or words after each sentence that tell what you think now. Did you change any answers? Put an **X** by each answer that you changed.

1.	Summer is cooler than spring.	True	Not True
2.	Summer has a lot of daylight hours.	True	Not True
3.	Many trees grow green leaves in summer.	True	Not True

Home Activity: Together talk about your child's answers. Have your child explain why his or her answers may have changed after reading the lesson.

Name ______________________________

Lesson 4 Review

Use with pages 182–183.

Complete the Sentence

Write the word that completes each sentence.

Summer	families	vegetables	Temperature

1. ______________ is how warm or cold something is.

2. ______________ can have hot days and warm nights.

3. You can see many animal ______________ in the summer.

4. Some ______________ grow well in the summer.

Predict

5. Complete the chart by drawing a tree in the summer.

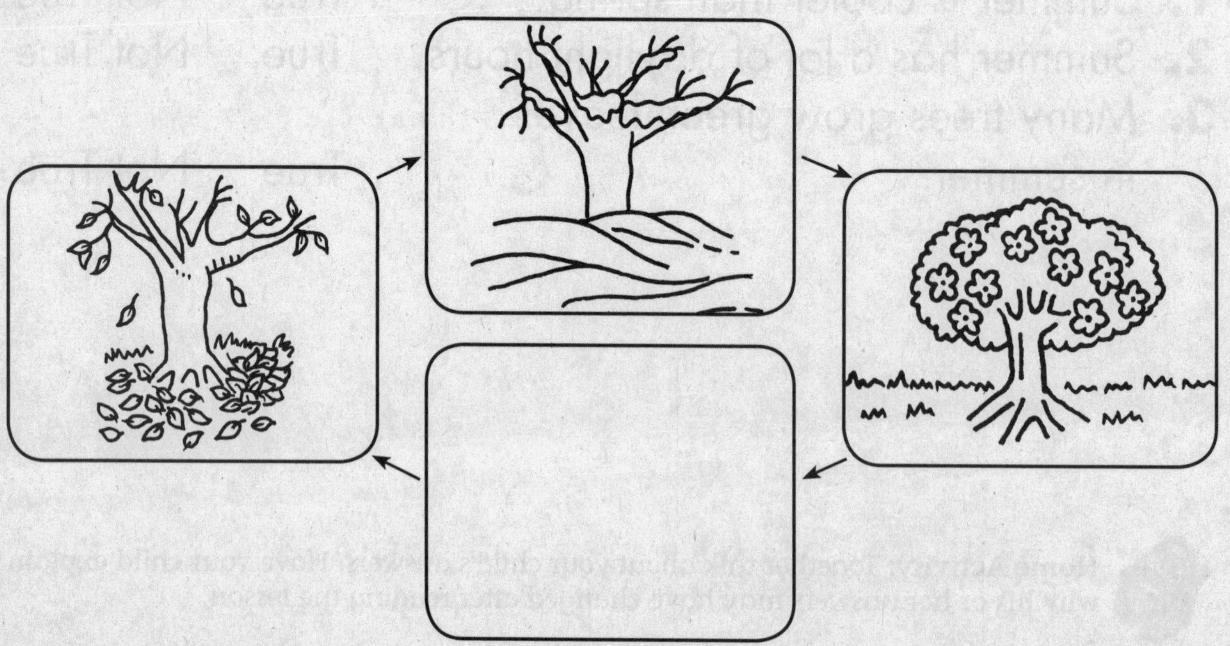

Name ______________________________

Use with pages 184–185.

What is fall?

Before You Read Lesson 5

Read each sentence. Do you think it is true? Do you think it is not true? Circle the word or words after each sentence that tell what you think.

1. Fall is cooler than summer. True Not True
2. Fall has more daylight hours than summer. True Not True
3. Some animals start to get ready for the winter. True Not True

After You Read Lesson 5

Read each sentence again. Circle the word or words after each sentence that tell what you think now. Did you change any answers? Put an **X** by each answer that you changed.

1. Fall is cooler than summer. True Not True
2. Fall has more daylight hours than summer. True Not True
3. Some animals start to get ready for the winter. True Not True

Home Activity: Together talk about your child's answers. Have your child explain why his or her answers may have changed after reading the lesson.

Name ______________________

Use with pages 184–185.

Complete the Sentence

Write the word that completes each sentence.

fall	gather	harvest	migrate

1. It gets cooler, and leaves turn colors in ______________.
2. Farmers gather, or ______________, their crops.
3. Some animals ______________ food for winter in the fall.
4. Some animals ______________ to warmer places.

Picture Clues

5. What does fall look like? Color the picture of fall. Then draw something you like to do in fall.

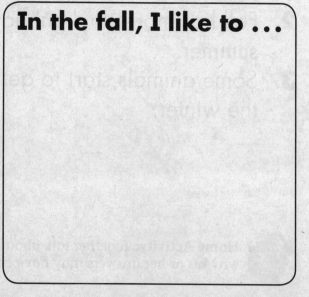

In the fall, I like to . . .

Name ___________________________

Use with pages 186–187.

What is winter?

Before You Read Lesson 6

Read each sentence. Do you think it is true? Do you think it is not true? Circle the word or words after each sentence that tell what you think.

1.	Winter is colder than fall.	True	Not True
2.	Leaves change color in the winter.	True	Not True
3.	Some animals sleep through the winter.	True	Not True

After You Read Lesson 6

Read each sentence again. Circle the word or words after each sentence that tell what you think now. Did you change any answers? Put an **X** by each answer that you changed.

1.	Winter is colder than fall.	True	Not True
2.	Leaves change color in the winter.	True	Not True
3.	Some animals sleep through the winter.	True	Not True

Home Activity: Together talk about your child's answers. Have your child explain why his or her answers may have changed after reading the lesson.

Name ______________________________

Use with pages 186–187.

Complete the Sentence

Write the word that completes each sentence.

winter	hibernate	leaves	snows

1. In some places, it is very cold in ______________.

2. In some places, it ______________ in winter.

3. Many trees have no ______________ in winter.

4. Bears and other animals ______________, or have a long, deep sleep.

Picture Clues

5. Which season is it? Match the picture with the season.

spring summer fall winter

______________	______________
______________	______________

Name ______________________________

Use with pages 188–193.

What are some kinds of bad weather?

Before You Read Lesson 7

Read each sentence. Do you think it is true? Do you think it is not true? Circle the word or words after each sentence that tell what you think.

1.	A thunderstorm has lightning.	True	Not True
2.	Tornadoes are hard to predict.	True	Not True
3.	Tornadoes have heavy rains but no winds.	True	Not True
4.	Hurricanes have strong winds but no rain.	True	Not True

After You Read Lesson 7

Read each sentence again. Circle the word or words after each sentence that tell what you think now. Did you change any answers? Put an **X** by each answer that you changed.

1.	A thunderstorm has lightning.	True	Not True
2.	Tornadoes are hard to predict.	True	Not True
3.	Tornadoes have heavy rains but no winds.	True	Not True
4.	Hurricanes have strong winds but no rain.	True	Not True

Home Activity: Together talk about your child's answers. Have your child explain why his or her answers may have changed after reading the lesson.

Name ______________________________

Use with pages 188–193.

Complete the Sentence

Write the word that completes each sentence.

tornado	thunder	lightning	hurricane

1. A flash of light in the sky during a storm is __________.

2. The loud sound you hear during a storm is __________.

3. A __________ is a strong wind shaped like a funnel.

4. A __________ is a large storm that starts over water.

Draw Conclusions

5. Why do we need to learn how to be safe during storms?

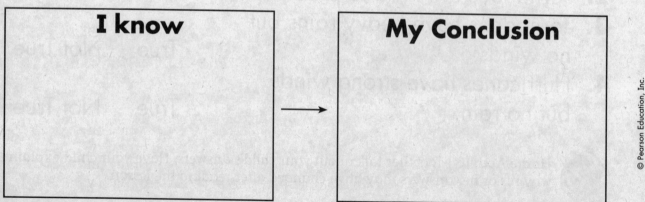

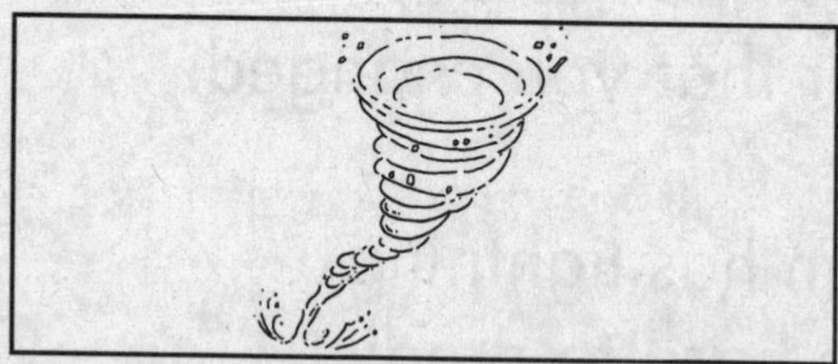

I know	→	My Conclusion

Name ________________________

Use with Chapter 6.

Weather Reports

Mr. Hanson's second-grade class did reports on kinds of bad weather. They made a graph to show how many students reported on each kind of bad weather.

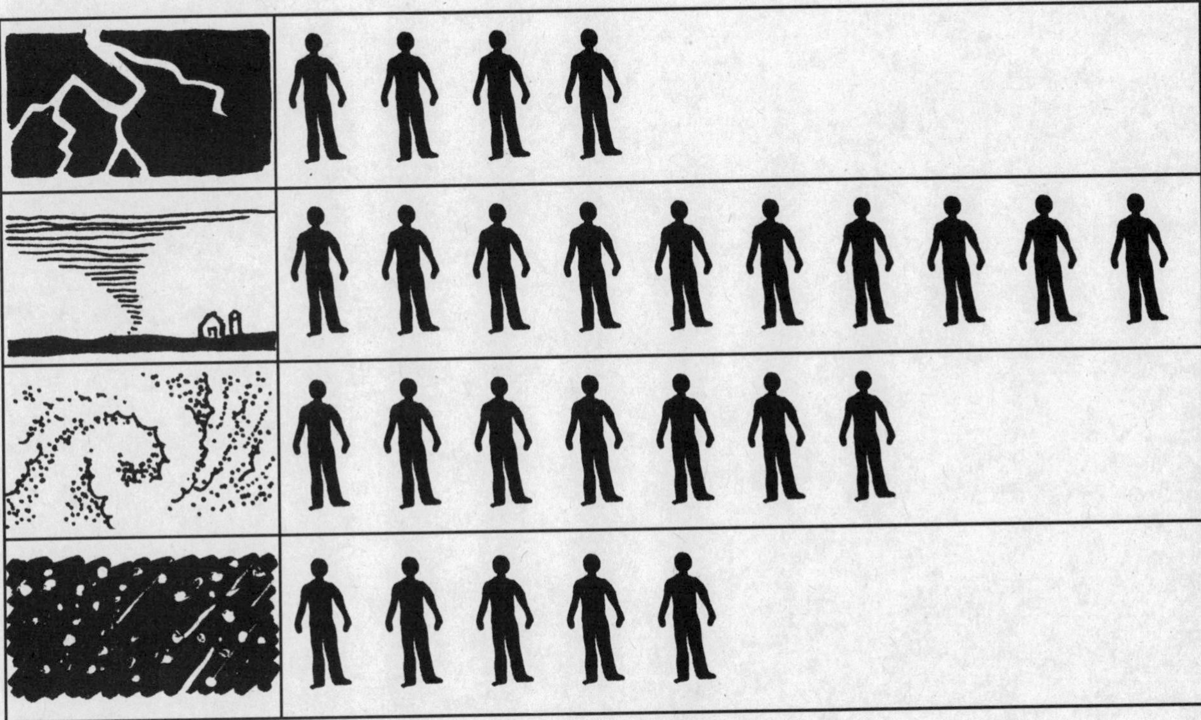

Look at the graph. Answer the questions.

1. How many students reported on hurricanes? ________

2. How many more students reported on tornadoes than on blizzards? ________________

3. Use <, >, or =. Compare how many students reported on thunderstorms to how many students reported on hurricanes. ______________

Directions: Look at the graph. Count how many students reported on each kind of bad weather. Use those numbers to answer the questions.
Home Activity: Your child learned how to use a graph. Ask family and friends which of the four kinds of bad weather they have experienced. With your child, make a graph like the one on the page to show the information.

Notes

Family Science Activity

Check the Weather Forecast

Materials:

- The daily weather forecast from a newspaper, television, or radio
- An outdoor thermometer
- Drawing paper
- Pen or pencil

Steps

1. Talk with your child about the daily weather forecast. Discuss what the forecast predicts for the next day, including temperature, precipitation, and how cloudy or sunny the day will be. Talk about how weather forecasters make their predictions.
2. Make a chart to record the weather forecast for the next seven days. The chart should have seven columns and two rows. Label the columns with the seven days, beginning with the day after you start the activity. Label the first row **The Weather Forecast**. Label the second row **The Weather Today**.
3. Check the weather forecast for tomorrow and write the forecasted temperature and other details in the first row. On the following day, observe the weather with your child and record it. Continue recording the forecasted weather and the actual weather for seven days.
4. After seven days, help your child compare the weather forecast and the actual weather for the week. Discuss how accurate the forecast was in predicting the weather. Talk about why it might be difficult to predict the weather.

Take Home Booklet

Use with Chapter 6.

Dear Family,

Your child is learning about patterns of weather and how the weather changes from season to season. In the science chapter Earth's Weather and Seasons, our class has learned about different kinds of weather and what weather is typical to each season. The children have also learned about thunderstorms, hurricanes, and tornadoes, and what to do to stay safe in these kinds of dangerous weather.

In addition to learning how weather can affect plants and animals, the children have also learned many new vocabulary words. Help your child to make these words a part of his or her own vocabulary by using them when you talk together about weather and the seasons.

water cycle
evaporate
condense
migrate
hibernate
lightning
tornado
hurricane

These following pages include activities that you and your child can do together. By participating in your child's education, you will help to bring the learning home.

Weather and Art

What do you do when it rains? When it is warm and sunny? When it is very cold? Pick one kind of weather. Draw a picture of yourself in that weather. Write about the picture.

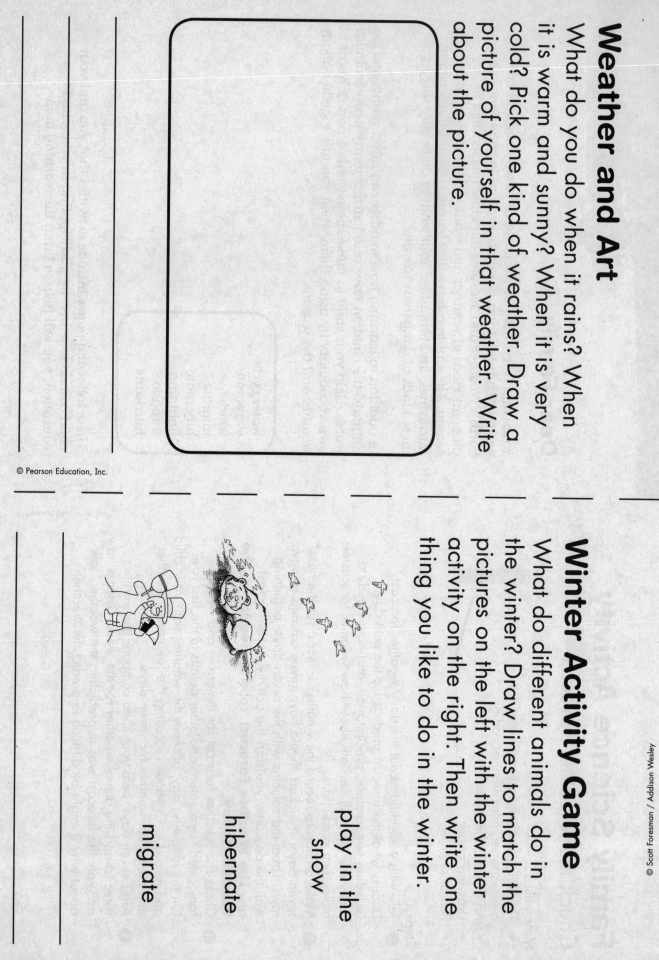

Winter Activity Game

What do different animals do in the winter? Draw lines to match the pictures on the left with the winter activity on the right. Then write one thing you like to do in the winter.

play in the snow

hibernate

migrate

Name ____________________

Use with Chapter 7.

Draw a picture or write a sentence to go with each word.

dinosaur	fossil
extinct	paleontologist

Directions: Read the words and draw pictures to illustrate them or write sentences about them. Cut out the boxes to use as word cards.
Home Activity: Have your child pretend to be a paleontologist and explain what he or she does using all the vocabulary words.

Use with Chapter 7.

Retell

Trilobite

Millions of years ago, this small animal lived in Earth's oceans. It had a shell and three body parts. The middle part had many legs.

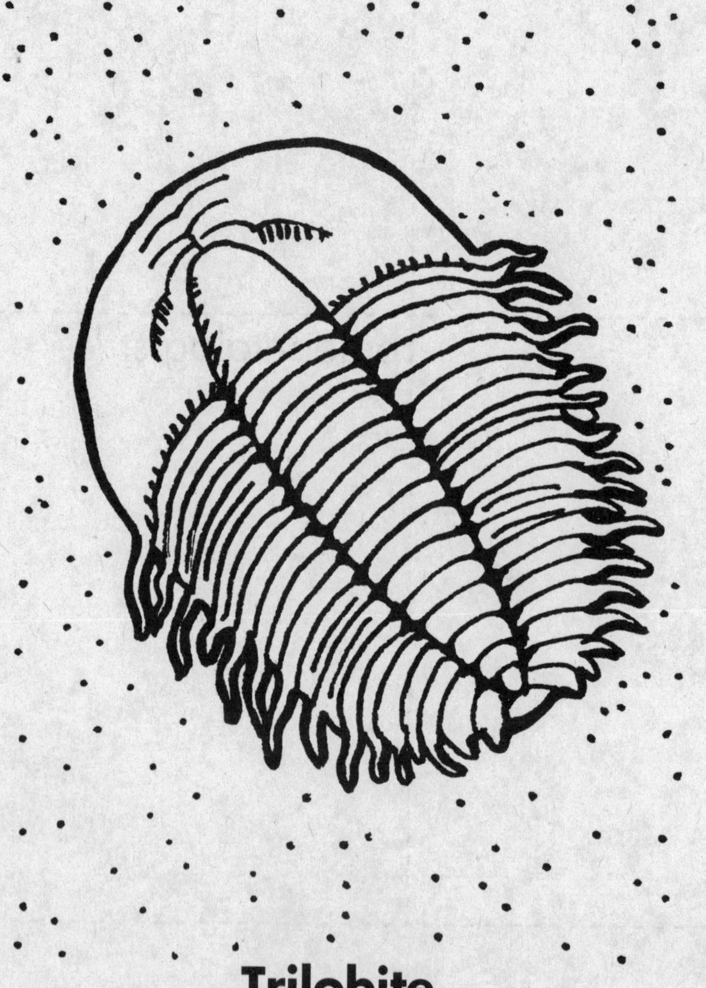

Trilobite

Name ______________________________

Use with Chapter 7.

Apply It!

Communicate Suppose someone asked you about this animal. Write what you would tell the person about the animal. Use your own words.

Retell

Directions: Read the Science Story and look at the picture. Then write the facts you learned about the trilobite in the *Retell* boxes before you retell the facts to a partner.
Home Activity: Your child learned about the skill of retelling. Read a short storybook to your child. Then ask your child to retell the story in his or her own words.

Notes

Name ______________________________

Use with pages 207–209.

How can we learn about the past?

Before You Read Lesson 1

Read each sentence. Do you think it is true? Do you think it is not true? Circle the word or words after each sentence that tell what you think.

1.	Fossils were once plants or animals.	True	Not True
2.	Fossils form very quickly.	True	Not True
3.	Paleontologists study fossils.	True	Not True

After You Read Lesson 1

Read each sentence again. Circle the word or words after each sentence that tell what you think now. Did you change any answers? Put an **X** by each answer that you changed.

1.	Fossils were once plants or animals.	True	Not True
2.	Fossils form very quickly.	True	Not True
3.	Paleontologists study fossils.	True	Not True

Home Activity: Together talk about your child's answers. Have your child explain why his or her answers may have changed after reading the lesson.

Name ______________________

Use with pages 207–209.

Complete the Sentence

Write the word that completes each sentence.

fossil	shapes	bones	paleontologist

1. The print of a plant or animal from many years ago is a ____________.

2. A ____________ is a scientist who studies fossils.

3. Some fossils are very old ____________.

4. Some fossils are ____________ that have been left in rocks.

Retell

5. How are fossils formed?

Fossils come from . . .

____

____

____

____

____

____

____

Name ______________________

Use with pages 210–211.

What can we learn from fossils?

Before You Read Lesson 2

Read each sentence. Do you think it is true? Do you think it is not true? Circle the word or words after each sentence that tell what you think.

1.	Fossils give clues about long-ago living things.	True	Not True
2.	Extinct animals have disappeared from Earth forever.	True	Not True
3.	Only animals can become extinct.	True	Not True

After You Read Lesson 2

Read each sentence again. Circle the word or words after each sentence that tell what you think now. Did you change any answers? Put an **X** by each answer that you changed.

1.	Fossils give clues about long-ago living things.	True	Not True
2.	Extinct animals have disappeared from Earth forever.	True	Not True
3.	Only animals can become extinct.	True	Not True

Home Activity: Together talk about your child's answers. Have your child explain why his or her answers may have changed after reading the lesson.

Name ______________________________

Lesson 2 Review

Use with pages 210–211.

Complete the Sentence

Write the word that completes each sentence.

fossil	extinct	habitat	past

1. Fossils give us clues about the ____________.

2. A ____________ shows us how plants and animals looked many years ago.

3. A plant or animal that no longer lives on Earth is ____________.

4. Sometimes a ____________ can no longer meet an animal's needs.

Picture Clues

5. Color the pictures of fossils.

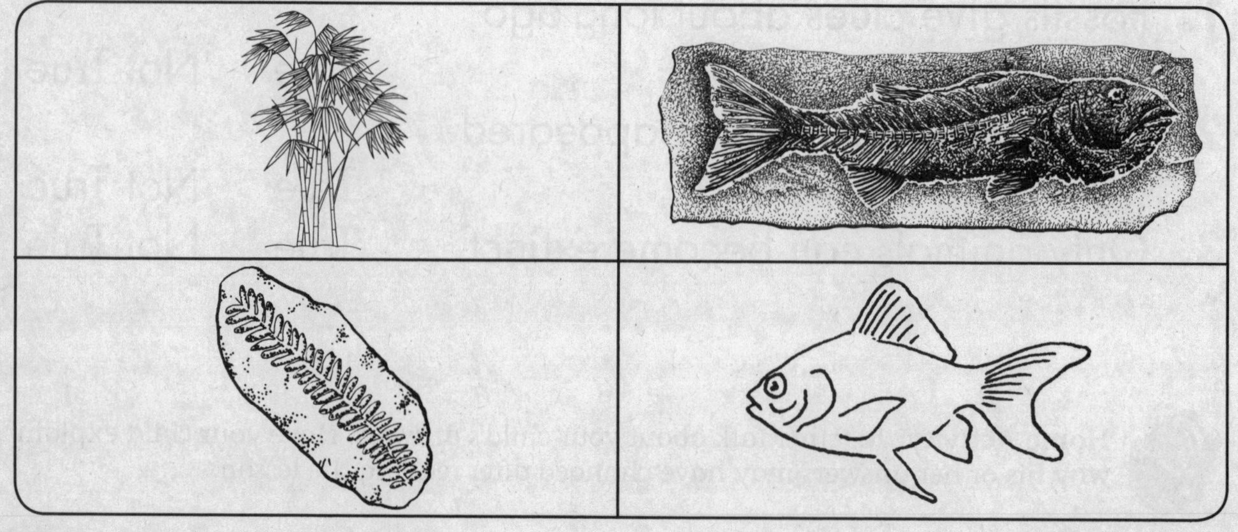

Name ___________________________________

Use with pages 212–215.

What were dinosaurs like?

Before You Read Lesson 3

Read each sentence. Do you think it is true? Do you think it is not true? Circle the word or words after each sentence that tell what you think.

1.	Not all dinosaurs are extinct.	True	Not True
2.	Dinosaurs with big, flat teeth ate plants.	True	Not True
3.	Some dinosaurs ate other dinosaurs.	True	Not True

After You Read Lesson 3

Read each sentence again. Circle the word or words after each sentence that tell what you think now. Did you change any answers? Put an **X** by each answer that you changed.

1.	Not all dinosaurs are extinct.	True	Not True
2.	Dinosaurs with big, flat teeth ate plants.	True	Not True
3.	Some dinosaurs ate other dinosaurs.	True	Not True

Home Activity: Together talk about your child's answers. Have your child explain why his or her answers may have changed after reading the lesson.

Name ______________________________

Lesson 3 Review

Use with pages 212–215.

Complete the Sentence

Write the word that completes each sentence.

Dinosaurs	All	Fossils	Stegosaurus

1. ______________ lived long ago.

2. ______________ dinosaurs are extinct.

3. ______________ are proof of how animals and plants looked long ago.

4. A ______________ had a small head and mouth.

Retell

5. Dinosaurs lived a long time ago. Tell one fact you know about dinosaurs.

Dinosaurs were . . .

____

____

____

____

____

____

Name ______________________

Use with pages 216–217.

What are some new discoveries?

Before You Read Lesson 4

Read each sentence. Do you think it is true? Do you think it is not true? Circle the word or words after each sentence that tell what you think.

1.	Oviraptors were one kind of dinosaur.	True	Not True
2.	Oviraptors laid eggs.	True	Not True
3.	Oviraptors ate their own eggs.	True	Not True

After You Read Lesson 4

Read each sentence again. Circle the word or words after each sentence that tell what you think now. Did you change any answers? Put an **X** by each answer that you changed.

1.	Oviraptors were one kind of dinosaur.	True	Not True
2.	Oviraptors laid eggs.	True	Not True
3.	Oviraptors ate their own eggs.	True	Not True

Home Activity: Together talk about your child's answers. Have your child explain why his or her answers may have changed after reading the lesson.

Name ______________________________

Lesson 4 Review

Use with pages 216–217.

Complete the Sentence

Write the word that completes each sentence.

Oviraptor	eggs	predator	Discoveries

1. An ______________ was a small dinosaur that protected its eggs.

2. A ______________ is something that catches and eats other animals.

3. ______________ are new things we learn.

4. Oviraptors kept their ______________ safe.

Draw Conclusions

5. Why do we study dinosaurs and fossils?

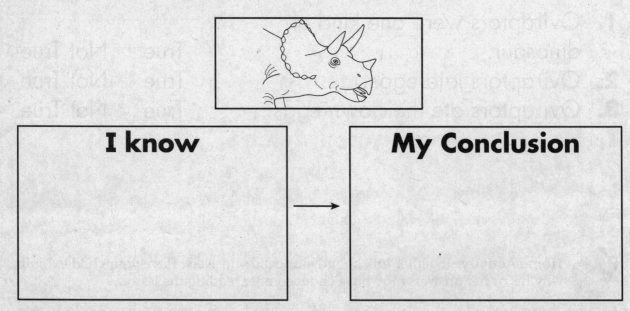

I know	→	My Conclusion

Notes

Name ________________________________

Use with Chapter 7.

How long are dinosaur teeth?

Look at the dinosaur teeth. Estimate how long each tooth is. Measure the teeth.
Fill in the bar graph to show how long each dinosaur tooth is. Use the bar graph to answer the questions.

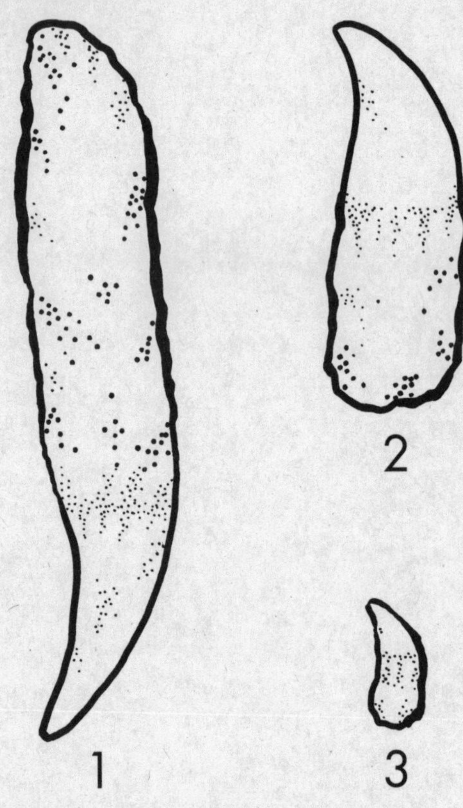

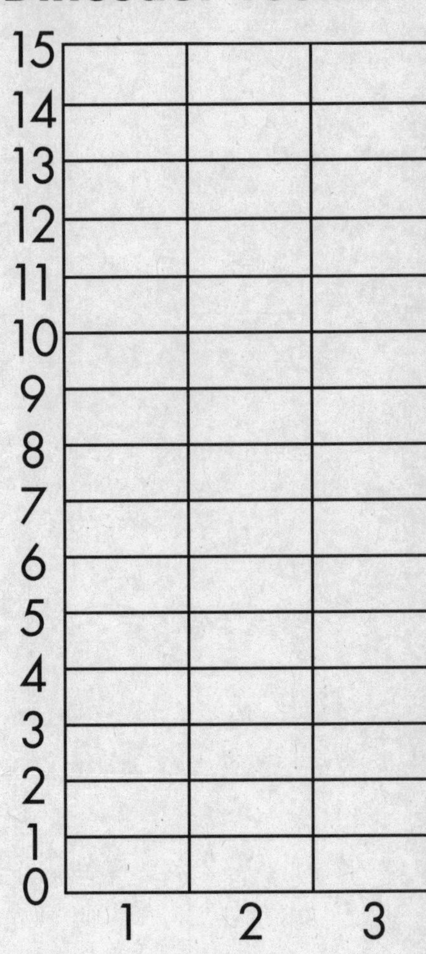

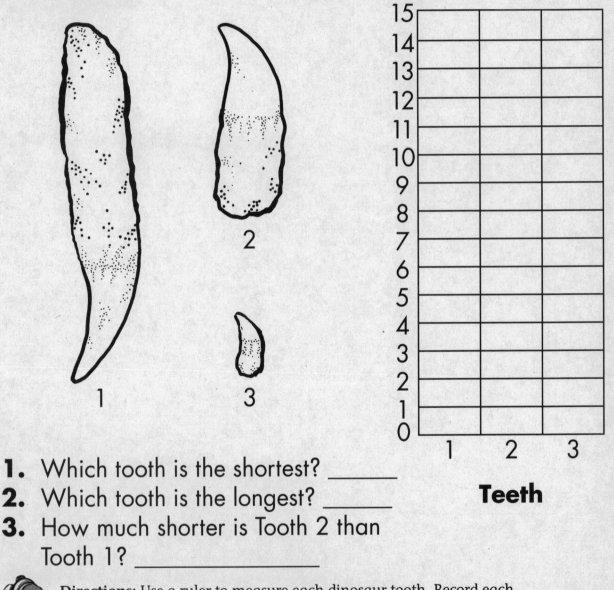

1. Which tooth is the shortest? ______

2. Which tooth is the longest? ______

3. How much shorter is Tooth 2 than Tooth 1? ________________

Directions: Use a ruler to measure each dinosaur tooth. Record each measurement by filling in the appropriate number of boxes in the graph. Use the information in the graph to answer the questions.
Home Activity: Your child learned how to record data on a bar graph. Have your child measure middle fingers on family members' hands and record the measurements on a bar graph like the one on the page.

Family Science Activity

Leaf Fossils

Materials:

- Three leaves, each from a different plant
- Clay
- Waxed paper
- Rolling pin
- Pencil

Steps

1. Talk with your child about how fossils are formed. Discuss the different kinds of fossils they have seen.
2. Help your child form three flat pieces of clay, about one half inch thick. Make sure the pieces of clay are bigger than the leaves.
3. Place a leaf face down on a piece of clay and cover it with a sheet of waxed paper.
4. Help your child press the leaf into the clay using a rolling pin. Remove the waxed paper and the leaf. Repeat with the other two leaves and pieces of clay.
5. Talk about how the leaves and the fossils you made of them are alike and how they are different.
6. Put the pieces of clay in a safe place to dry. Encourage your child to show and discuss the leaf fossils with family members and friends.

Use with Chapter 7.

Dear Family,

Your child is learning about fossils and dinosaurs. In the science chapter Fossils and Dinosaurs, our class has learned what fossils can tell us about the past. The children have also learned how fossils are formed and what dinosaurs were like.

In addition to learning about different kinds of dinosaurs, the children have also learned many new vocabulary words. Help your child to make these words a part of his or her own vocabulary by using them when you talk together about fossils and dinosaurs.

fossil
extinct
paleontologist
dinosaur

These following pages include activities that you and your child can do together. By participating in your child's education, you will help to bring the learning home.

Dinosaur Words

How many words can you make from the name of a dinosaur? Look at the dinosaur name below. Look at the two words that are spelled with letters from this name. Then, write three more words that use letters from the name of this dinosaur.

TRICERATOPS

RAT

STOP

Science and Art

What is your favorite dinosaur? Did it walk, fly, or swim? How big was it? What did it eat? Draw a picture of the dinosaur in the box below. Then, write two sentences that tell about this dinosaur.

Name ______________________________

Use with Chapter 8.

Draw a picture or write a sentence to go with each word.

states of matter	property
liquid	gas
solid	mass
mixture	

Directions: Read the words and draw pictures to illustrate them or write sentences about them. Cut out the boxes to use as word cards.
Home Activity: Ask your child to identify the words that name states of matter *(gas, liquid, solid)* and then explain how *mass, property,* and *mixture* are related to matter.

Name ______________________

Use with Chapter 8.

Draw Conclusions

Read the science activity and look at the pictures.

Science Activity
Place some ice in a clear cup. Put the cup in the sun or another warm spot in the room. Observe what happens. Record the results in your science journal.

Apply It!

Infer Use the chart on the next page. Write what you know. Write what you conclude.

Name ______________________________

Use with Chapter 8.

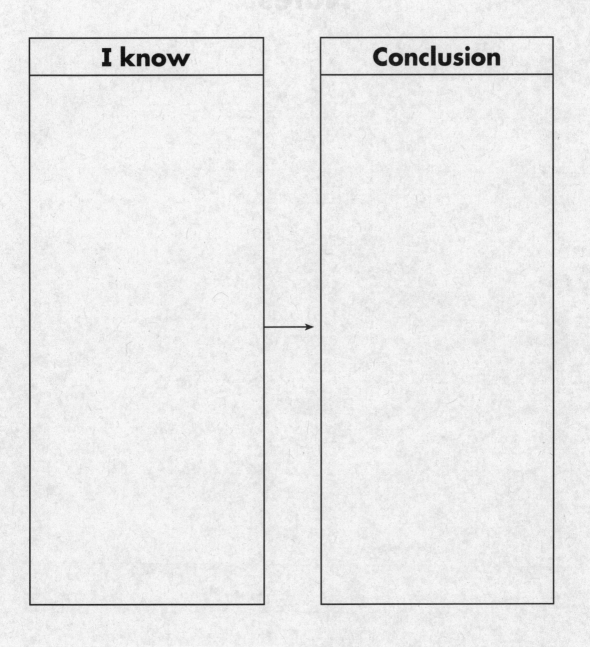

I know	Conclusion

Directions: What do you think will happen? Write what you know in the *I know* box. Then write your conclusion in the *Conclusion* box.
Home Activity: Your child learned about drawing conclusions. Have your child add an ice cube to a glass of hot water and another to a glass of room temperature water. Ask your child to predict which cube will melt first. Discuss the results.

Notes

Name ____________________

Use with pages 239–241.

What is matter?

Before You Read Lesson 1

Read each sentence. Do you think it is true? Do you think it is not true? Circle the word or words after each sentence that tell what you think.

1. Matter has mass and uses up space. True Not True
2. Properties of matter cannot be observed. True Not True
3. Size is a property of matter. True Not True

After You Read Lesson 1

Read each sentence again. Circle the word or words after each sentence that tell what you think now. Did you change any answers? Put an **X** by each answer that you changed.

1. Matter has mass and uses up space. True Not True
2. Properties of matter cannot be observed. True Not True
3. Size is a property of matter. True Not True

Home Activity: Together talk about your child's answers. Have your child explain why his or her answers may have changed after reading the lesson.

Name ___________________________

Lesson 1 Review

Use with pages 239–241.

Complete the Sentence

Write the word that completes each sentence.

mass	matter	property	parts

1. Anything that takes up space and has weight is ______________.

2. The amount of matter in an object is its ______________.

3. Matter is made of very small ______________.

4. The way something looks, sounds, tastes, smells, or feels is a ______________.

Draw Conclusions

5. Are people made up of matter? Do they have mass? Explain.

I know	→	My Conclusion

Name ______________________________

Use with pages 242–247.

What are the states of matter?

Before You Read Lesson 2

Read each sentence. Do you think it is true? Do you think it is not true? Circle the word or words after each sentence that tell what you think.

1.	A solid has its own shape and size.	True	Not True
2.	You measure liquids with a ruler.	True	Not True
3.	Gas takes up all the space inside its container.	True	Not True

After You Read Lesson 2

Read each sentence again. Circle the word or words after each sentence that tell what you think now. Did you change any answers? Put an **X** by each answer that you changed.

1.	A solid has its own shape and size.	True	Not True
2.	You measure liquids with a ruler.	True	Not True
3.	Gas takes up all the space inside its container.	True	Not True

Home Activity: Together talk about your child's answers. Have your child explain why his or her answers may have changed after reading the lesson.

Name ___________________________

Use with pages 242–247.

Complete the Sentence

Write the word or phrase that completes each sentence.

solid	liquid	gas	states of matter

1. There are three ______________.
2. Water is a ______________.
3. A book is a ______________.
4. Air is a ______________.

Infer

5. Draw a picture of a solid and a liquid.

Name ______________________________

Use with pages 248–251.

How can matter be changed?

Before You Read Lesson 3

Read each sentence. Do you think it is true? Do you think it is not true? Circle the word or words after each sentence that tell what you think.

1.	The shape of matter does not change.	True	Not True
2.	Parts of a mixture do not change.	True	Not True
3.	Salt water is a mixture.	True	Not True

After You Read Lesson 3

Read each sentence again. Circle the word or words after each sentence that tell what you think now. Did you change any answers? Put an **X** by each answer that you changed.

1.	The shape of matter does not change.	True	Not True
2.	Parts of a mixture do not change.	True	Not True
3.	Salt water is a mixture.	True	Not True

Home Activity: Together talk about your child's answers. Have your child explain why his or her answers may have changed after reading the lesson.

Name ______________________________

Use with pages 248–251.

Complete the Sentence

Write the word that completes each sentence.

mixture	salad	separate	changed

1. Matter can be ______________ in many ways.

2. When you put several different things together, you make a ______________.

3. You can ______________ a mixture to see its parts.

4. A ______________ is an example of a mixture.

Draw Conclusions

5. Is this a mixture? Why or why not?

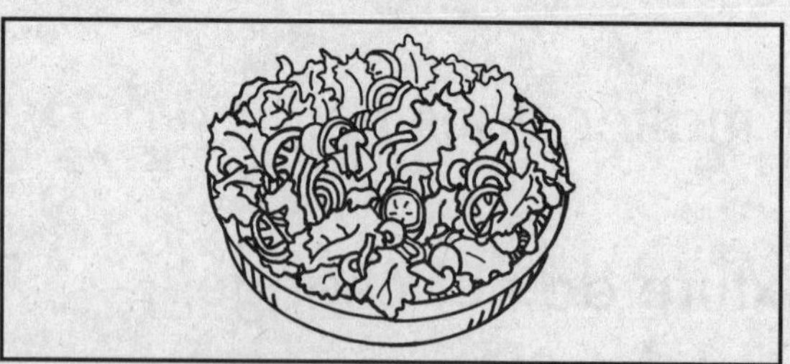

I know	→	My Conclusion

Name ______________________________

Use with pages 252–255.

How can cooling and heating change matter?

Before You Read Lesson 4

Read each sentence. Do you think it is true? Do you think it is not true? Circle the word or words after each sentence that tell what you think.

1.	To change the state of matter, change the temperature.	True	Not True
2.	Cold can change a solid to a liquid.	True	Not True
3.	Heat can change a liquid to a gas.	True	Not True

After You Read Lesson 4

Read each sentence again. Circle the word or words after each sentence that tell what you think now. Did you change any answers? Put an **X** by each answer that you changed.

1.	To change the state of matter, change the temperature.	True	Not True
2.	Cold can change a solid to a liquid.	True	Not True
3.	Heat can change a liquid to a gas.	True	Not True

Home Activity: Together talk about your child's answers. Have your child explain why his or her answers may have changed after reading the lesson.

Name ______________________________

Use with pages 252–255.

Complete the Sentence

Write the word that completes each sentence.

solid	matter	melt	gases

1. Water is ______________.

2. Ice is ______________ water.

3. Heat can change liquids to ______________.

4. Ice and snow ______________ when air warms.

Predict

5. What will happen to the ice in this glass?

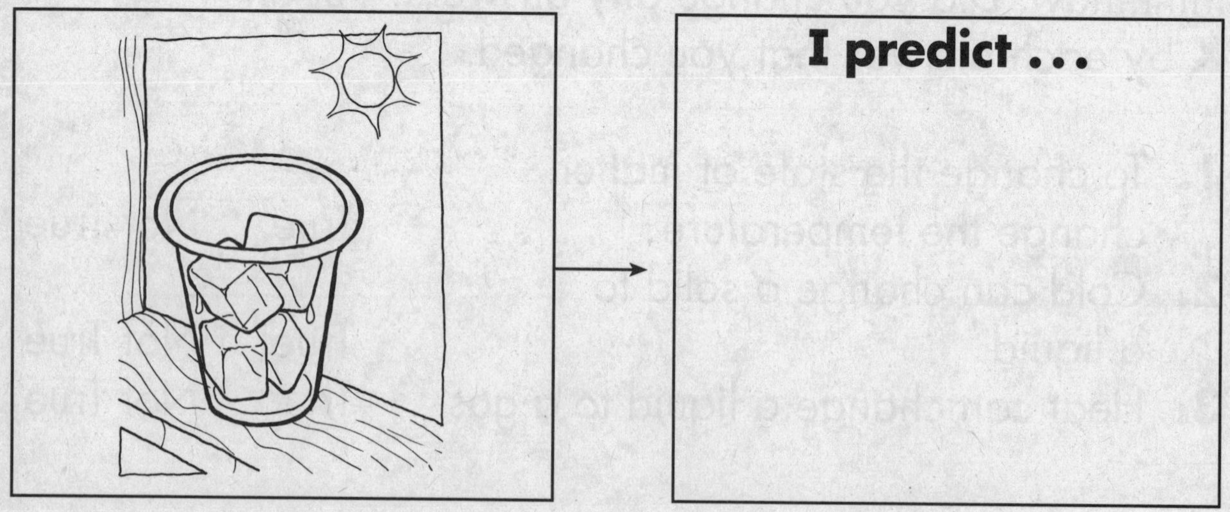

Name ______________________________

Use with Chapter 8.

Measuring Matter

Anna measured two solids and two liquids. Look at her measurements.

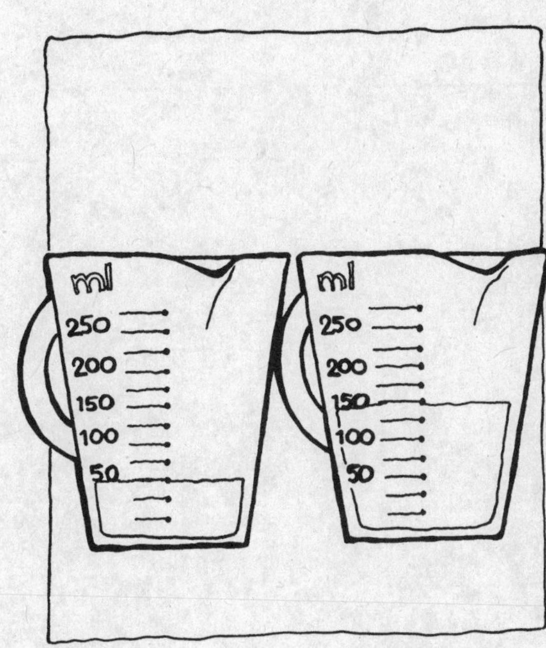

Record the data in the table for Anna.

My Measurements

Length of Pencils	Volume of Water
Pencil 1. ______ cm	Cup 1. ______ mL
Pencil 2. ______ cm	Cup 2. ______ mL

Directions: Look at the measuring tools. Tell what the lengths and volumes are. Write them in the chart.
Home Activity: Your child learned to read measures of length and volume. Ask your child to explain how to use a ruler and a measuring cup. Then have him or her measure the length of a spoon and the volume a favorite glass holds.

Notes

Family Science Activity

Separating Salt and Water

Materials:

- Glass jar
- Hot water
- Salt
- Spoon
- Pencil
- String
- Nail

Steps

1. Talk with your child about different kinds of mixtures you have around the house, such as salads or jars of coins. Discuss how you might separate each one into its parts.
2. Help your child make a mixture of water and salt by stirring salt into a jar filled with hot water. Add the salt to the water one spoonful at a time until no more salt will dissolve.
3. Discuss how you might now separate the salt and the water.
4. Tie one end of the string to the nail. Place the pencil on the mouth of the jar. Tie the string to the pencil so the nail hangs in the salt water.
5. Leave the jar uncovered in a warm place. Check the jar every day until all the water has evaporated and the salt has crystallized on the string.
6. Examine the crystals on the string. Talk about where the salt and water went when you separated the mixture. Compare the salt crystals on the string with the salt you stirred into the water. How are they alike? How are they different?

Take Home Booklet

Use with Chapter 8.

Dear Family,

Your child is learning that everything is made of matter. In the science chapter Properties of Matter, our class has learned about the three states of matter: solids, liquids, and gases. The children have also learned different ways that matter can be changed.

In addition to learning about matter, the children have also learned many new vocabulary words. Help your child to make these words a part of his or her own vocabulary by using them when you talk together about matter in its different states.

mass
property
states of matter
solid
liquid
gas
mixture

These following pages include activities that you and your child can do together. By participating in your child's education, you will help to bring the learning home.

Matching

Look at the pictures and words below. Draw lines to match each object on the left with a property it has.

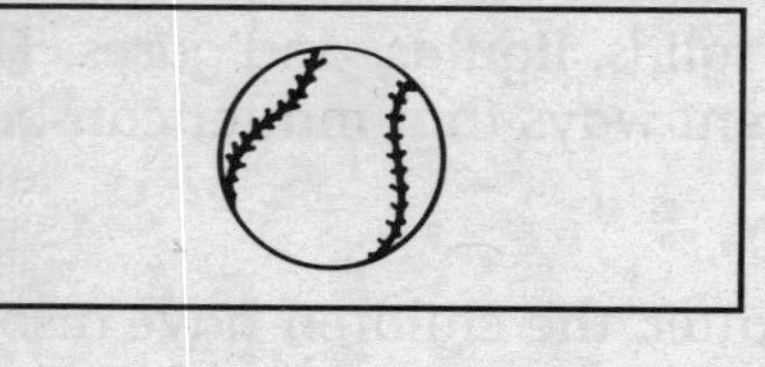

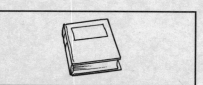

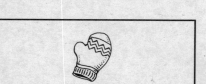

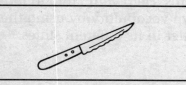

light

round

sharp

heavy

soft

Matter Crossword

Write each vocabulary word in the puzzle. One clue is the first letter of each word. Another clue is how many letters are in each word.

gas
liquid
mass
mixture
matter
property
solid
states

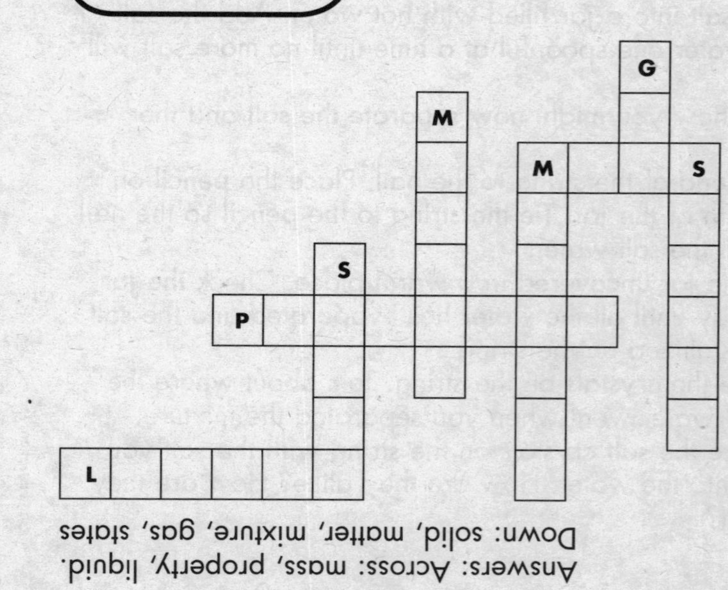

Answers: Across: mass, property, liquid.
Down: solid, matter, mixture, gas, states

Name ____________________

Use with Chapter 9.

Draw a picture or write a sentence to go with each word.

energy	solar energy
electricity	reflect
fuel	conduct

Directions: Read the words and draw pictures to illustrate them or write sentences about them. Cut out the boxes to use as word cards.
Home Activity: Ask your child to define *energy* and name at least five kinds of energy. Then ask questions that show how each of the other five terms above are related to energy. For example, ask *What kind of energy is reflected? What kind is conducted?*

Name ______________________________

Use with Chapter 9.

Infer

Read the science story.

Tina went inside when it began to rain. After the storm, the sun came out. Rays of sunlight shone through the mist. Then Tina saw a rainbow. She counted seven separate colors.

Apply It!

Infer What caused the rainbow? Use the chart on the next page. Write what you know. Write what you can infer.

Name ______________________________

Use with Chapter 9.

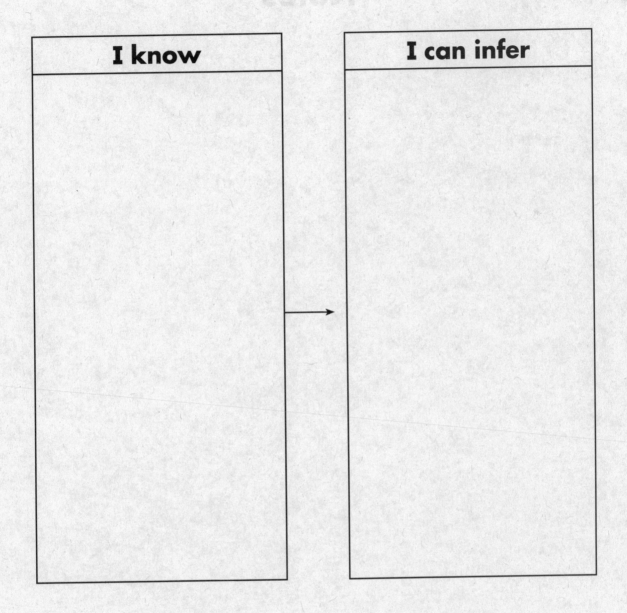

I know		I can infer
	→	

Directions: Write what you know from the picture and the story in the *I know* box. Think about what this information allows you to infer. Write the answer to the question in the *I can infer* box.

Home Activity: Your child learned about making inferences. Find a newspaper or magazine article with a picture. Read it together, and then ask your child a question that can be answered by thinking about the information in the picture and the article.

Notes

Use with pages 271–273.

What is energy?

Before You Read Lesson 1

Read each sentence. Do you think it is true? Do you think it is not true? Circle the word or words after each sentence that tell what you think.

1. You do not use energy when you are asleep.	True	Not True
2. To change anything takes energy.	True	Not True
3. Most of our energy comes from the Sun.	True	Not True

After You Read Lesson 1

Read each sentence again. Circle the word or words after each sentence that tell what you think now. Did you change any answers? Put an **X** by each answer that you changed.

1. You do not use energy when you are asleep.	True	Not True
2. To change anything takes energy.	True	Not True
3. Most of our energy comes from the Sun.	True	Not True

Home Activity: Together talk about your child's answers. Have your child explain why his or her answers may have changed after reading the lesson.

Name ______________________________

Use with pages 271–273.

Complete the Sentence

Write the word or phrase that completes each sentence.

energy	solar energy	sunlight	Sun

1. The Sun gives us heat and light called ______________.

2. Everything you do uses ______________.

3. Earth gets most of its energy from the ______________.

4. People use ______________ to see in the daytime.

Picture Clues

5. Color the pictures that show energy being used.

Name ______________________________

Use with pages 274–277.

How do living things use energy?

Before You Read Lesson 2

Read each sentence. Do you think it is true? Do you think it is not true? Circle the word or words after each sentence that tell what you think.

1.	Animals get energy from food.	True	Not True
2.	Food energy helps you grow.	True	Not True
3.	Rice and pasta have a lot of vitamins.	True	Not True

After You Read Lesson 2

Read each sentence again. Circle the word or words after each sentence that tell what you think now. Did you change any answers? Put an **X** by each answer that you changed.

1.	Animals get energy from food.	True	Not True
2.	Food energy helps you grow.	True	Not True
3.	Rice and pasta have a lot of vitamins.	True	Not True

Home Activity: Together talk about your child's answers. Have your child explain why his or her answers may have changed after reading the lesson.

Name ______________________

Use with pages 274–277.

Complete the Sentence

Write the word or phrase that completes each sentence.

grow	energy	play	food groups

1. Animals use energy to move, live, and ____________.
2. Food gives you energy to work and ____________.
3. People need ____________.
4. The things you should eat every day fit into five ____________.

Infer

5. Eric only ate one vegetable this week. Is this a good idea? Why or why not?

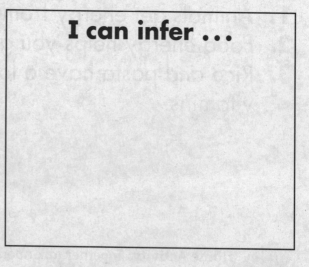

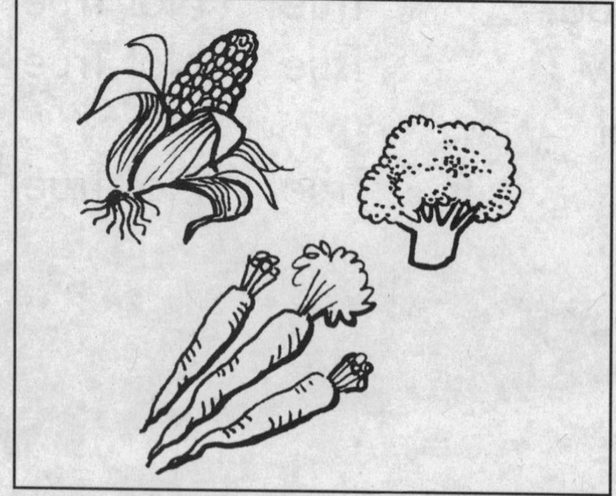

I can infer . . .

Name ______________________________

Use with pages 278–281.

What are some sources of heat?

Before You Read Lesson 3

Read each sentence. Do you think it is true? Do you think it is not true? Circle the word or words after each sentence that tell what you think.

1.	Gas and oil are fuels used for heat.	True	Not True
2.	A conductor is something you burn.	True	Not True
3.	Heat moves from hot to cold.	True	Not True

After You Read Lesson 3

Read each sentence again. Circle the word or words after each sentence that tell what you think now. Did you change any answers? Put an **X** by each answer that you changed.

1.	Gas and oil are fuels used for heat.	True	Not True
2.	A conductor is something you burn.	True	Not True
3.	Heat moves from hot to cold.	True	Not True

Home Activity: Together talk about your child's answers. Have your child explain why his or her answers may have changed after reading the lesson.

Name ______________________

Use with pages 278–281.

Complete the Sentence

Write the word that completes each sentence.

source	fuel	conductor	heat

1. The place something comes from is its ____________.

2. Fire is a source of ____________.

3. We burn ____________ to make heat.

4. Heat moves easily through a ____________, such as a metal pan.

Infer

5. Color the pictures that show good conductors.

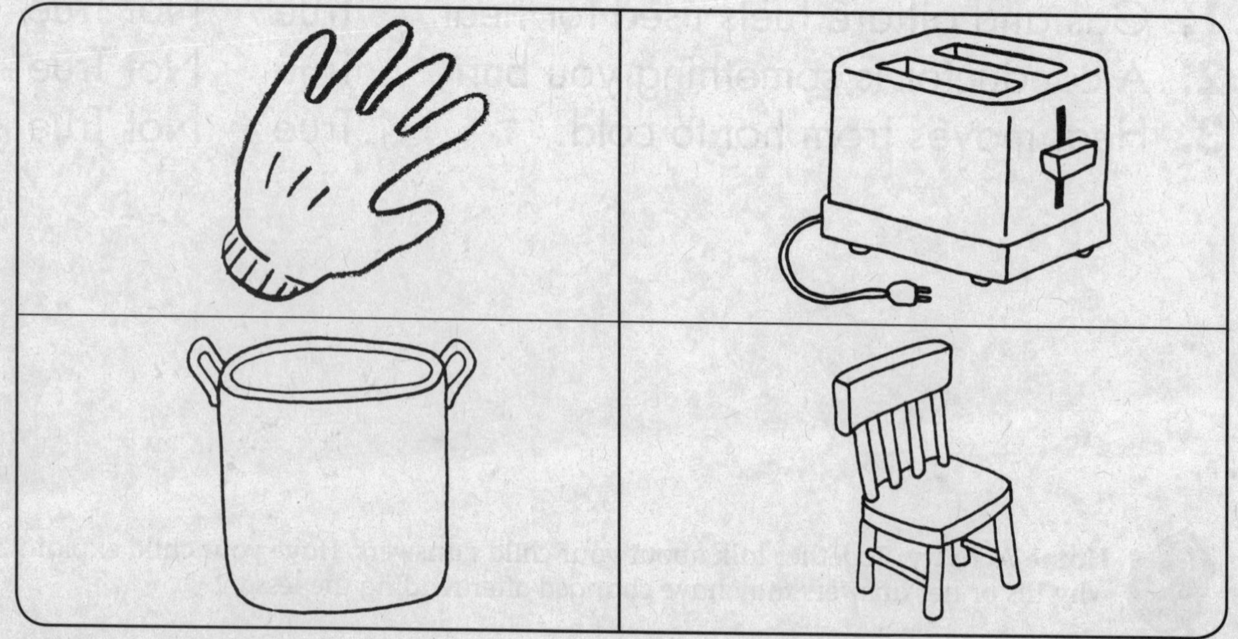

Name ___________________________

Use with pages 282–285.

How does light move?

Before You Read Lesson 4

Read each sentence. Do you think it is true? Do you think it is not true? Circle the word or words after each sentence that tell what you think.

1.	Light is a form of energy.	True	Not True
2.	Reflected light causes shadows.	True	Not True
3.	Shadows are shortest at noon.	True	Not True
4.	Dark colors reflect light best.	True	Not True

After You Read Lesson 4

Read each sentence again. Circle the word or words after each sentence that tell what you think now. Did you change any answers? Put an **X** by each answer that you changed.

1.	Light is a form of energy.	True	Not True
2.	Reflected light causes shadows.	True	Not True
3.	Shadows are shortest at noon.	True	Not True
4.	Dark colors reflect light best.	True	Not True

Home Activity: Together talk about your child's answers. Have your child explain why his or her answers may have changed after reading the lesson.

Name ____________________

Use with pages 282–285.

Complete the Sentence

Write the word that completes each sentence.

reflects	light	shadow	rainbow

1. One form of energy is __________.

2. Light __________ when it bounces off something smooth and shiny.

3. Raindrops in the air bend sunlight and make a __________.

4. When something blocks the light, it makes a __________.

Infer

5. It is going to be a very hot day. Which shirt should you wear? Why?

I will wear . . .

Name ______________________________

Use with pages 286–289.

What are other kinds of energy?

Before You Read Lesson 5

Read each sentence. Do you think it is true? Do you think it is not true? Circle the word or words after each sentence that tell what you think.

1.	Sound is a kind of energy.	True	Not True
2.	Electricity is energy of motion.	True	Not True
3.	You should not use electricity near water.	True	Not True

After You Read Lesson 5

Read each sentence again. Circle the word or words after each sentence that tell what you think now. Did you change any answers? Put an **X** by each answer that you changed.

1.	Sound is a kind of energy.	True	Not True
2.	Electricity is energy of motion.	True	Not True
3.	You should not use electricity near water.	True	Not True

Home Activity: Together talk about your child's answers. Have your child explain why his or her answers may have changed after reading the lesson.

Name ______________________

Use with pages 286–289.

Complete the Sentence

Write the word that completes each sentence.

electricity	energy	safely	wind

1. Motion and sound are kinds of __________.

2. The energy used to move a sailboat is __________.

3. A form of energy that uses a plug or batteries is __________.

4. It is important to use electricity __________.

Infer

5. Why shouldn't you play near power lines?

I can infer . . .

Name ________________________________

Make a Data Chart

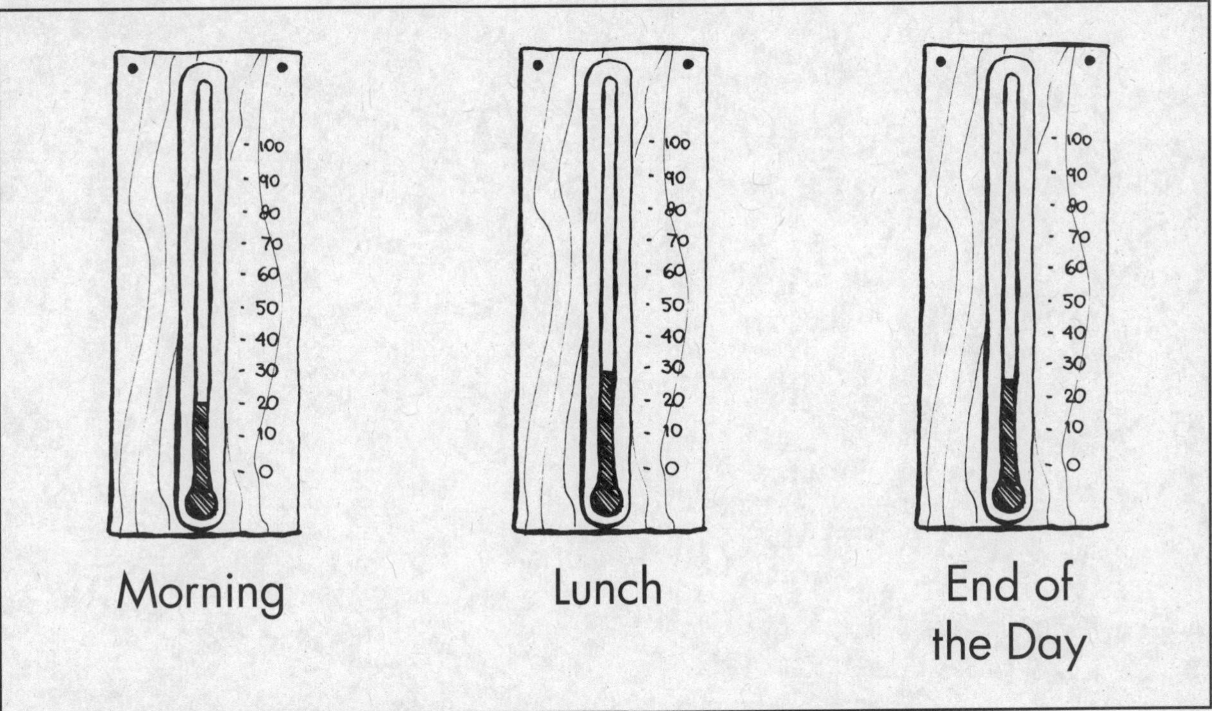

Write the temperatures in the chart. Circle the hottest time of day.

Changing Temperatures

Time of Day	morning	lunch	end of day
Temperature			

Directions: The temperature changes through the day. Read the thermometers. Then fill in the data chart. Circle the time of day when we get the most solar energy.

Home Activity: Your child learned to make a data chart. Together find how many kilowatts (electric energy) you used at home in the last four months. (Your bill shows this data.) Make a data chart like the one on this page. Talk about any pattern you see.

Notes

Family Science Activity

Make a Sundial

Materials:
- 9″ x 9″ cardboard sheet
- Pencil
- Clay
- Compass
- Watch or clock
- Pen or marker

Steps
1. Explain that a sundial can be used to tell the time of day, based on the ways shadows change during the day.
2. Stick a small ball of clay in the center of the cardboard. Press the pencil's eraser into the clay; the pencil should stand upright.
3. Write an *N* at the top of the cardboard. Label the remaining sides with an *S*, *W*, and *E* accordingly. Then, place the sundial outside, in direct sunlight. Use the compass to find north. Adjust the sundial so that *N* faces north.
4. Check the sundial every hour. Help your child make a mark on the cardboard where the pencil's shadow ends. Write the hour below this mark. At the end of the day, discuss how the shadows were longest in the morning; shortest at noon, and how they grow longer until sunset.

Use with Chapter 9.

Dear Family,

Your child is learning about energy. In the science chapter Energy, our class has learned where energy comes from and how it is used. The children have also learned about other kinds of energy, such as solar energy.

In addition to learning about why energy is important, the children have also learned many new vocabulary words. Help your child to make these words a part of his or her own vocabulary by using them when you talk together about energy.

energy
solar energy
source
fuel
conductor
reflect
shadow

The following pages include activities that you and your child can do together. By participating in your child's education, you will help to bring the learning home.

Energy Art

Draw a picture that shows one way that you use energy. Write a sentence about your picture on the lines below.

Kinds of Energy

Draw lines to match the pictures on the left with the kinds of energy on the right.

electricity

solar

food

wind

sound

Name ______________________

Use with Chapter 10.

Draw a picture or write a sentence to go with each word.

motion	force
gravity	work
friction	simple machine
attract	repel

Directions: Read the words and draw pictures to illustrate them or write sentences about them. Cut out the boxes to use as word cards.
Home Activity: Have your child tell how the terms *motion*, *force*, and *work* are related. Then have them compare and contrast the meanings of these pairs: *gravity/friction*, *work/simple machine*, *attract/repel*.

Name ______________________________

Use with Chapter 10.

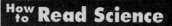

Put Things in Order

Read the science story.

Carlos and Mark had a heavy box to load. They could not lift it into their wagon. They found a board and leaned it against the end of the wagon. Then they pushed the box up their ramp.

Apply It!

Number the pictures on the next page in order.

Name ______________________________

Use with Chapter 10.

Directions: Look at the pictures. Write 1, 2, or 3 under each picture to put them in order.
Home Activity: Your child learned about putting events in 1-2-3 order. Ask your child to draw or explain what happens when he or she throws a basketball through a hoop. Help your child write the steps, using the words *first*, *next*, and *last*.

Notes

Name ______________________________

Use with pages 303–307.

How do objects move?

Before You Read Lesson 1

Read each sentence. Do you think it is true? Do you think it is not true? Circle the word or words after each sentence that tell what you think.

1.	Motion cannot be circular.	True	Not True
2.	Kicking a ball is applying force.	True	Not True
3.	More force makes an object move slower.	True	Not True
4.	Gravity pulls things toward Earth.	True	Not True

After You Read Lesson 1

Read each sentence again. Circle the word or words after each sentence that tell what you think now. Did you change any answers? Put an **X** by each answer that you changed.

1.	Motion cannot be circular.	True	Not True
2.	Kicking a ball is applying force.	True	Not True
3.	More force makes an object move slower.	True	Not True
4.	Gravity pulls things toward Earth.	True	Not True

Home Activity: Together talk about your child's answers. Have your child explain why his or her answers may have changed after reading the lesson.

Name ____________________

Use with pages 303–307.

Complete the Sentence

Write the word that completes each sentence.

motion	force	gravity	move

1. When something moves, it has ____________.

2. Objects can ____________ in different ways.

3. A ____________ makes something move.

4. The force that pulls things toward Earth is ____________.

Put Things in Order

5. Draw two pictures to show what happens first and last.

Brett throws a ball to Liz. The ball flies through the air.
Then Liz catches the ball.

Name ______________________________

Use with pages 308–309.

What is work?

Before You Read Lesson 2

Read each sentence. Do you think it is true? Do you think it is not true? Circle the word or words after each sentence that tell what you think.

1.	Opening a door is doing work.	True	Not True
2.	Pushing against a wall is doing work.	True	Not True
3.	Work makes objects move.	True	Not True

After You Read Lesson 2

Read each sentence again. Circle the word or words after each sentence that tell what you think now. Did you change any answers? Put an **X** by each answer that you changed.

1.	Opening a door is doing work.	True	Not True
2.	Pushing against a wall is doing work.	True	Not True
3.	Work makes objects move.	True	Not True

Home Activity: Together talk about your child's answers. Have your child explain why his or her answers may have changed after reading the lesson.

Name ______________________________

Use with pages 308–309.

Complete the Sentence

Write the word that completes each sentence.

work	amount	crayon	move

1. Whenever a force makes an object move, ______________ happens.

2. If something does not ______________, no work is done.

3. The ______________ of work you do depends on force and distance.

4. Pushing a ______________ across a desk is an example of work.

Infer

5. Color the pictures that show work being done.

Name ________________________________

Use with pages 310–313.

How can you change the way things move?

Before You Read Lesson 3

Read each sentence. Do you think it is true? Do you think it is not true? Circle the word or words after each sentence that tell what you think.

1.	More work moves an object further.	True	Not True
2.	Friction helps you do work.	True	Not True
3.	Friction heats up bicycle tires.	True	Not True

After You Read Lesson 3

Read each sentence again. Circle the word or words after each sentence that tell what you think now. Did you change any answers? Put an **X** by each answer that you changed.

1.	More work moves an object further.	True	Not True
2.	Friction helps you do work.	True	Not True
3.	Friction heats up bicycle tires.	True	Not True

Home Activity: Together talk about your child's answers. Have your child explain why his or her answers may have changed after reading the lesson.

Name ______________________

Lesson 3 Review

Use with pages 310–313.

Complete the Sentence

Write the word that completes each sentence.

friction	smooth	heavy	heat

1. It takes more force to move a ____________ object than a light one.

2. A force that makes moving objects slow down or stop is ____________.

3. Objects move faster on a ____________ surface than on grass.

4. Friction causes ____________.

Infer

5. Draw two things you could skate on that would cause different amounts of friction.

Less Friction	More Friction

Name ______________________

Use with pages 314–317.

How can simple machines help you do work?

Before You Read Lesson 4

Read each sentence. Do you think it is true? Do you think it is not true? Circle the word or words after each sentence that tell what you think.

1.	Any tool is a simple machine.	True	Not True
2.	Use a wedge to push things apart.	True	Not True
3.	A beaver uses its front teeth like a wedge to cut into wood.	True	Not True

After You Read Lesson 4

Read each sentence again. Circle the word or words after each sentence that tell what you think now. Did you change any answers? Put an **X** by each answer that you changed.

1.	Any tool is a simple machine.	True	Not True
2.	Use a wedge to push things apart.	True	Not True
3.	A beaver uses its front teeth like a wedge to cut into wood.	True	Not True

Home Activity: Together talk about your child's answers. Have your child explain why his or her answers may have changed after reading the lesson.

Name ______________________

Use with pages 314–317.

Complete the Sentence

Write the word or phrase that completes each sentence.

pulley	wedge	machine	simple machine

1. A ____________ is a tool that can do work.
2. A ____________ is a tool without many moving parts.
3. You can use a knife as a ____________ to help you push bread apart.
4. You can use a wheel and rope as a ____________ to help you lift something.

Put Things in Order

5. Read the story and number the pictures in order.

Mark and Andre try to lift a box into the car. They get a board to make an inclined plane. They push the box up the board.

Name ______________________________

Use with pages 318–321.

What are magnets?

Before You Read Lesson 5

Read each sentence. Do you think it is true? Do you think it is not true? Circle the word or words after each sentence that tell what you think.

1. The poles of a magnet have the strongest force. True Not True
2. Magnets placed N to S will repel. True Not True
3. Magnets can pick up iron objects. True Not True

After You Read Lesson 5

Read each sentence again. Circle the word or words after each sentence that tell what you think now. Did you change any answers? Put an **X** by each answer that you changed.

1. The poles of a magnet have the strongest force. True Not True
2. Magnets placed N to S will repel. True Not True
3. Magnets can pick up iron objects. True Not True

Home Activity: Together talk about your child's answers. Have your child explain why his or her answers may have changed after reading the lesson.

Name ______________________

Use with pages 318–321.

Complete the Sentence

Write the word that completes each sentence.

attract	magnet	repel	poles

1. A ____________ can push or pull some kinds of metal.

2. Two opposite poles will ____________, or pull toward each other.

3. Two like poles will ____________, or push away from each other.

4. The two ends of magnets are called ____________.

Predict

5. Draw two things a magnet attracts. Then draw two things a magnet does not attract.

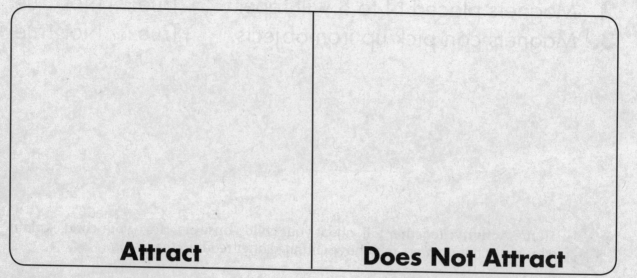

Attract	**Does Not Attract**

Name ______________________________

Use with Chapter 10.

Measuring Motion

Tonya and Li measured how far they could throw different kinds of balls. Look at their data chart.

Distance the Ball Was Thrown

Kind of Ball Thrown	Tonya	Li
football	20 meters	18 meters
baseball	25 meters	35 meters
tennis ball	21 meters	21 meters

Use the data chart to answer these questions.

1. Which ball did Tonya throw the farthest? ___________

2. How far did Li throw the tennis ball? ___________

3. How much farther did Tonya throw the football than Li threw it? Write a number sentence.

____

Directions: Study the chart. Use the data to answer the questions.
Home Activity: Your child learned about measuring and comparing distance moved. Measure how far your child can roll a toy vehicle across a rug, then across a wood, tile, or linoleum floor with one push. Compare the measurements and discuss the differences.

Notes

Family Science Activity

Mighty Magnets

Materials:
- 2 magnets
- Paper clips
- Paper
- Leaf
- Penny
- Pencil
- Nails

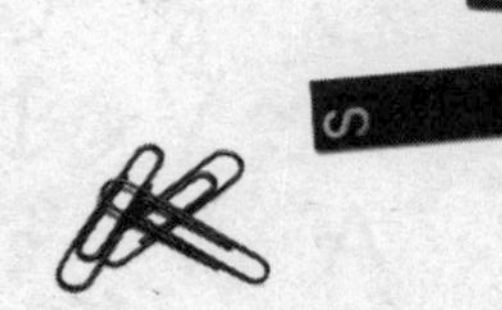

Steps

1. Give your child the magnets. Encourage your child to touch the ends, or poles, of each magnet together. Ask your child to identify poles that are alike and those that are different. Like poles will repel; the magnets will push away from each other. If opposite poles are put together, they attract; the magnets will pull toward each other.
2. Then, lay the remaining materials on a table. Encourage your child to touch the magnet to each item. Find out which of these objects the magnet will attract. Magnets attract some metal objects. Talk about why the remaining items were not attracted to the magnet.

Use with Chapter 10.

Dear Family,

Your child is learning about forces and the movement of objects. In the science chapter Forces and Motion, our class has learned that objects can move in different ways. The children have also learned about the six kinds of simple machines and how they help people do work.

In addition to learning about different ways forces can move objects, the children have also learned many new vocabulary words. Help your child to make these words a part of his or her own vocabulary by using them when you talk together about forces and motion.

motion
force
gravity
work
friction
simple machine
attract
repel

The following pages include activities that you and your child can do together. By participating in your child's education, you will help to bring the learning home.

Simple Machines

Circle the simple machines below.

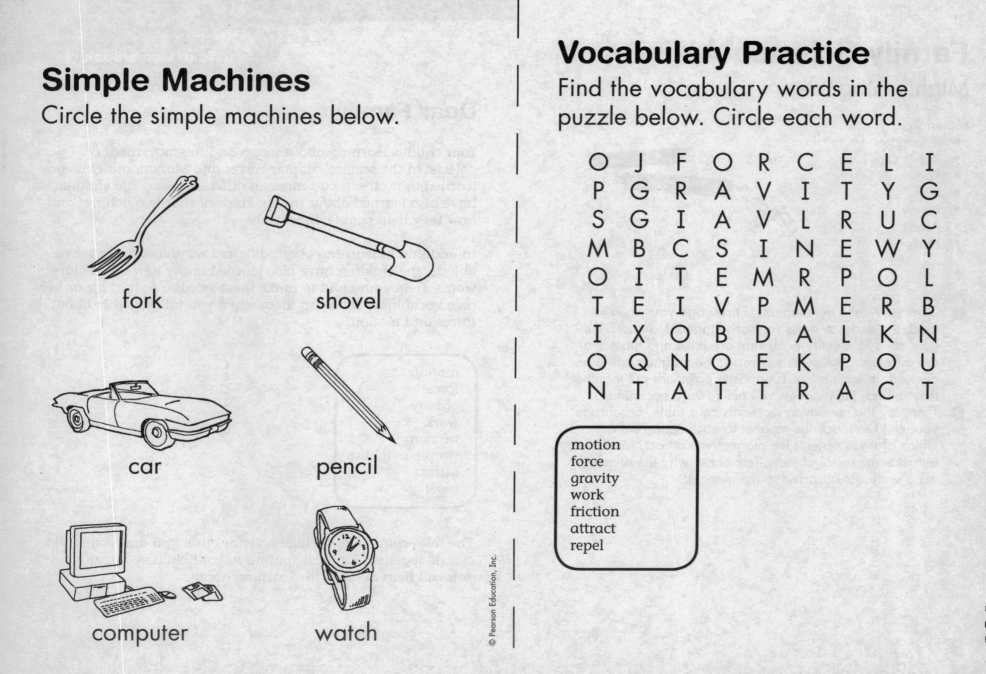

fork

shovel

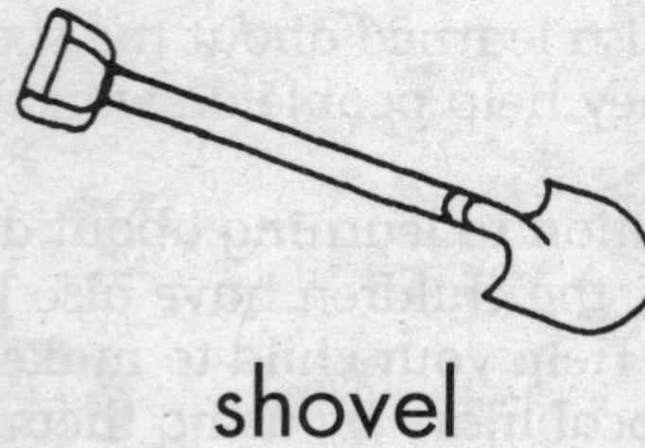

car

pencil

computer

watch

Vocabulary Practice

Find the vocabulary words in the puzzle below. Circle each word.

O	J	F	O	R	C	E	L	I
P	G	R	A	V	I	T	Y	G
S	G	I	A	V	L	R	U	C
M	B	C	S	I	N	E	W	Y
O	I	T	E	M	R	P	O	L
T	E	I	V	P	M	E	R	B
I	X	O	B	D	A	L	K	N
O	Q	N	O	E	K	P	O	U
N	T	A	T	T	R	A	C	T

motion
force
gravity
work
friction
attract
repel

Name ________________________

Use with Chapter 11.

Draw a picture or write a sentence to go with each word.

vibrate	loudness
pitch	

Directions: Read the words and draw pictures to illustrate them or write sentences about them. Cut out the boxes to use as word cards.
Home Activity: Fill a set of four glasses to different levels with water. Have your child strike each glass with a fork and use this setup to demonstrate and explain the meanings of *vibrate*, *loudness*, and *pitch* and relate them to the concept of sound.

Name ______________________

Use with Chapter 11.

Important Details

Read the science article and look at the picture.

Pitch

The pitch of music can be high or low. An instrument with a short pipe, like a flute, has a high pitch. An instrument with tight strings, like a violin, also has a high pitch. An instrument with a long pipe or loose strings has a low pitch. Two instruments with low pitch are a bass and a trombone.

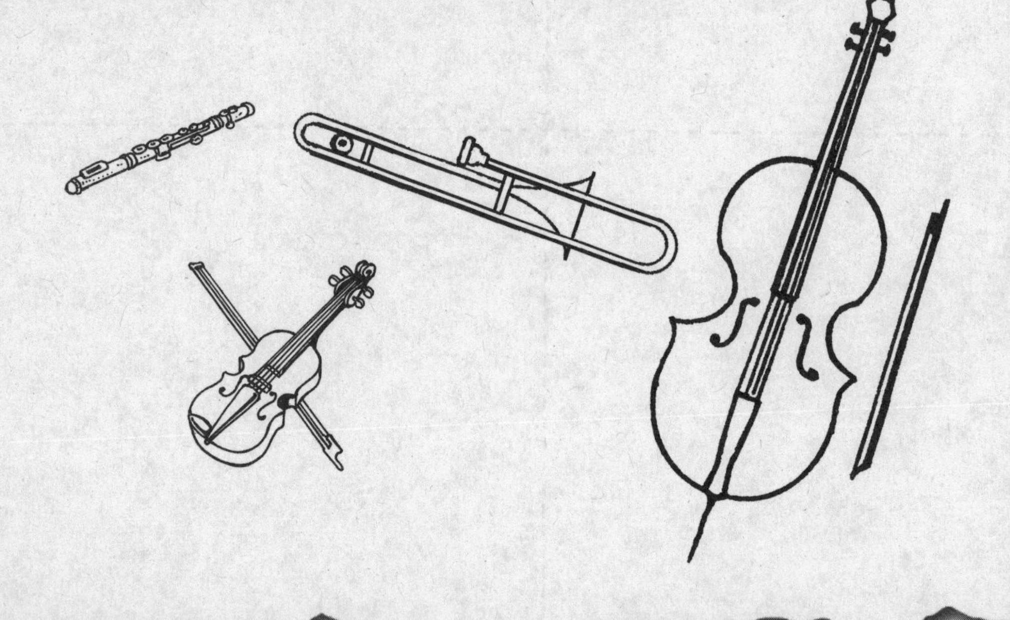

Name ______________________________

Use with Chapter 11.

Apply It!

What instruments have a high pitch? Look for the words that tell you. Use the chart below.

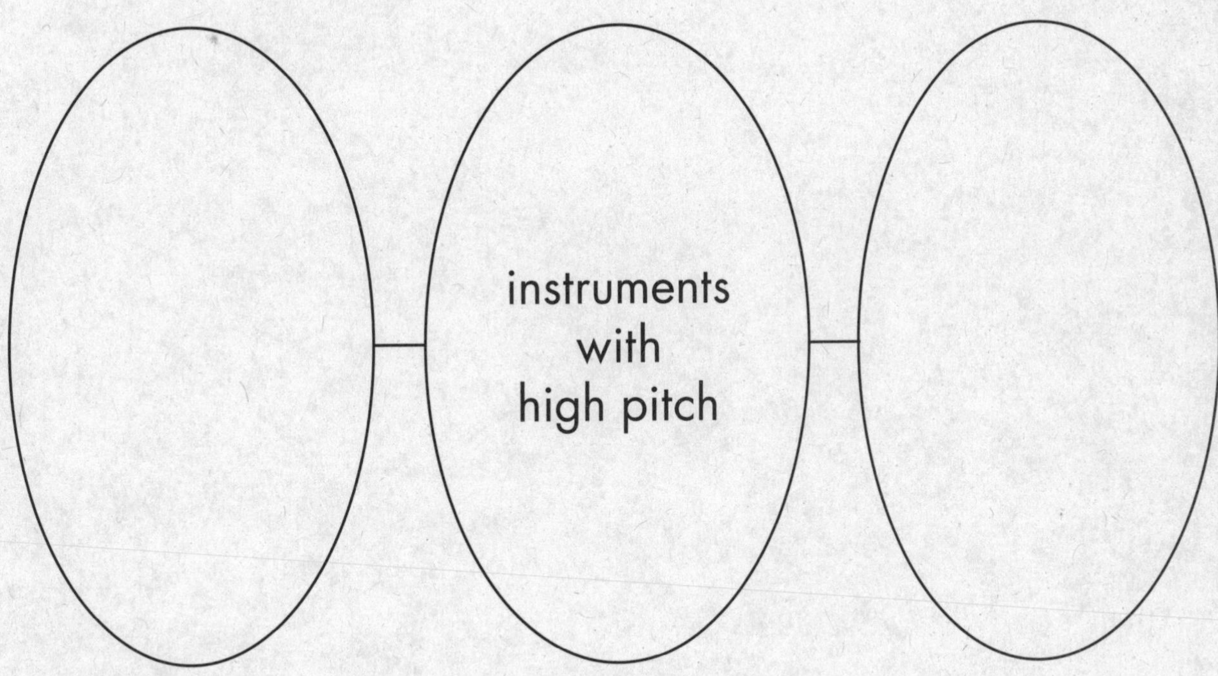

Directions: Read the Science Article and look at the picture. Then answer the question by filling in the diagram.
Home Activity: Your child learned to read for important details. Together, read a magazine or newspaper article. Make up a question about a key subject in the article. Ask your child to point out some important details about this subject.

Notes

Name ______________________

Use with pages 335–337.

What is sound?

Before You Read Lesson 1

Read each sentence. Do you think it is true? Do you think it is not true? Circle the word or words after each sentence that tell what you think.

1. A bell rings because it vibrates. True Not True
2. To vibrate is to move back and forth. True Not True
3. Hit something hard to make a soft sound. True Not True

After You Read Lesson 1

Read each sentence again. Circle the word or words after each sentence that tell what you think now. Did you change any answers? Put an **X** by each answer that you changed.

1. A bell rings because it vibrates. True Not True
2. To vibrate is to move back and forth. True Not True
3. Hit something hard to make a soft sound. True Not True

Home Activity: Together talk about your child's answers. Have your child explain why his or her answers may have changed after reading the lesson.

Name ______________________________

Use with pages 335–337.

Complete the Sentence

Write the word that completes each sentence.

vibrate	loudness	air	instruments

1. Musical ______________ make sounds when they are played.

2. To move quickly back and forth is to ______________.

3. Instruments make ______________ vibrate.

4. A sound's ______________ is how loud or soft it is.

Important Details

5. Draw three things that make soft sounds.

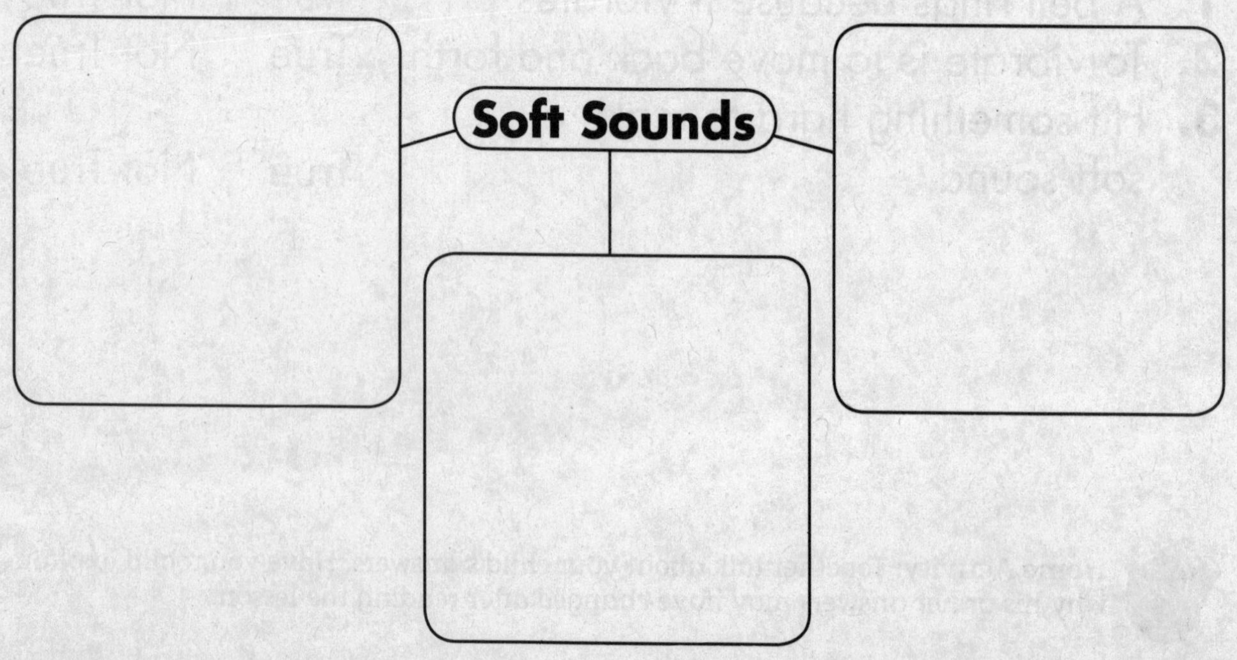

Name ____________________

Use with pages 338–339.

What is pitch?

Before You Read Lesson 2

Read each sentence. Do you think it is true? Do you think it is not true? Circle the word or words after each sentence that tell what you think.

1. A bird makes sounds with a low pitch. True Not True
2. A nearly full bottle has a high pitch. True Not True
3. A slow-vibrating object has a low-pitched sound. True Not True

After You Read Lesson 2

Read each sentence again. Circle the word or words after each sentence that tell what you think now. Did you change any answers? Put an **X** by each answer that you changed.

1. A bird makes sounds with a low pitch. True Not True
2. A nearly full bottle has a high pitch. True Not True
3. A slow-vibrating object has a low-pitched sound. True Not True

Home Activity: Together talk about your child's answers. Have your child explain why his or her answers may have changed after reading the lesson.

Name ______________________

Use with pages 338–339.

Complete the Sentence

Write the word that completes each sentence.

pitch	bird	bottle	bullfrog

1. A ______________ makes a sound with a high pitch.

2. A ______________ makes a sound with a low pitch.

3. A sound's ______________ is how high or low it is.

4. Air vibrates and makes a sound when you blow across a ______________.

Put in Order

5. Put these bottles in order from the lowest pitch (1) to the highest pitch (3).

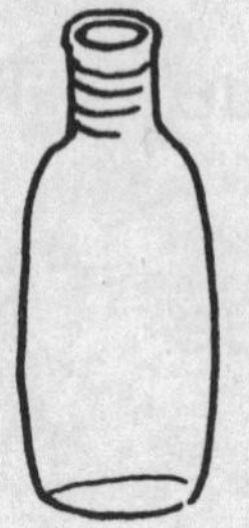
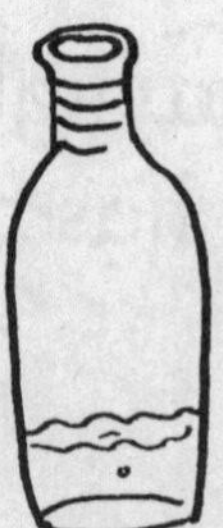

______________ ______________ ______________

Name ______________________

Use with pages 340–341.

How does sound travel?

Before You Read Lesson 3

Read each sentence. Do you think it is true? Do you think it is not true? Circle the word or words after each sentence that tell what you think.

1.	Sound moves fastest through solids.	True	Not True
2.	Sound moves slowest through gases.	True	Not True
3.	Sound does not move through liquids.	True	Not True

After You Read Lesson 3

Read each sentence again. Circle the word or words after each sentence that tell what you think now. Did you change any answers? Put an **X** by each answer that you changed.

1.	Sound moves fastest through solids.	True	Not True
2.	Sound moves slowest through gases.	True	Not True
3.	Sound does not move through liquids.	True	Not True

Home Activity: Together talk about your child's answers. Have your child explain why his or her answers may have changed after reading the lesson.

Name ________________________________

Lesson 3 Review

Use with pages 340–341.

Complete the Sentence

Write the word that completes each sentence.

sound	solids	air	moves

1. A form of energy you can hear is ____________.

2. Sound ____________ through solids, liquids, and gases.

3. Sounds travels faster through liquids than it does through ____________.

4. Sounds travels fastest through ____________.

Infer

5. Sound travels at different speeds through different objects. Write the words *solid*, *liquid*, and *gas* to show the order sound travels through them.

Fast	Faster	Fastest
____________	____________	____________

Name ______________________________

Use with pages 342–343.

How do some animals make sound?

Before You Read Lesson 4

Read each sentence. Do you think it is true? Do you think it is not true? Circle the word or words after each sentence that tell what you think.

1. Cricket sound comes from vibrating wings. True Not True
2. A lobster rubs its antenna along its head for sound. True Not True
3. A rattlesnake sounds like maracas. True Not True

After You Read Lesson 4

Read each sentence again. Circle the word or words after each sentence that tell what you think now. Did you change any answers? Put an **X** by each answer that you changed.

1. Cricket sound comes from vibrating wings. True Not True
2. A lobster rubs its antenna along its head for sound. True Not True
3. A rattlesnake sounds like maracas. True Not True

Home Activity: Together talk about your child's answers. Have your child explain why his or her answers may have changed after reading the lesson.

Name ______________________________

Lesson 4 Review

Use with pages 342–343.

Complete the Sentence

Write the word or phrase that completes each sentence.

many	rattlesnake	cricket	spiny lobster

1. Animals make sound in __________ ways.

2. A __________ makes sounds like a guitar by rubbing its wings together.

3. A __________ makes sounds like maracas by shaking the rattle in its tail.

4. A __________ makes sounds like a violin by rubbing its antenna against its head.

Alike and Different

5. How are a rattlesnake and a spiny lobster alike? How are they different?

Alike	Different

Name ___________________________

Use with pages 344–345.

What are sounds around you?

Before You Read Lesson 5

Read each sentence. Do you think it is true? Do you think it is not true? Circle the word or words after each sentence that tell what you think.

1.	Sounds are always around you.	True	Not True
2.	Dripping water is a soft sound.	True	Not True
3.	A police siren is a soft sound.	True	Not True

After You Read Lesson 5

Read each sentence again. Circle the word or words after each sentence that tell what you think now. Did you change any answers? Put an **X** by each answer that you changed.

1.	Sounds are always around you.	True	Not True
2.	Dripping water is a soft sound.	True	Not True
3.	A police siren is a soft sound.	True	Not True

Home Activity: Together talk about your child's answers. Have your child explain why his or her answers may have changed after reading the lesson.

Name ______________________________

Lesson 5 Review

Use with pages 344–345.

Complete the Sentence

Write the word that completes each sentence.

Vibrate	Loudness	Pitch	Sound

1. ______________ is a kind of energy we can hear.
2. ______________ is air moving back and forth.
3. ______________ is how high or low a sound is.
4. ______________ is how loud or soft a sound is.

Predict

5. Draw four ways you will make sounds today. Include two soft sounds and two loud sounds.

Soft Sounds	Loud Sounds

Name ______________________________

Use with Chapter 11.

Read a Bar Graph

People and animals can hear sounds with different pitches. Look at the graph. It shows units of vibration per second. A high-pitched sound has a high number. A low-pitched sound has a low number. Different organisms hear a different range of pitches.

Pitch of Sounds People and Animals Can Hear, in Units of Vibration per Second

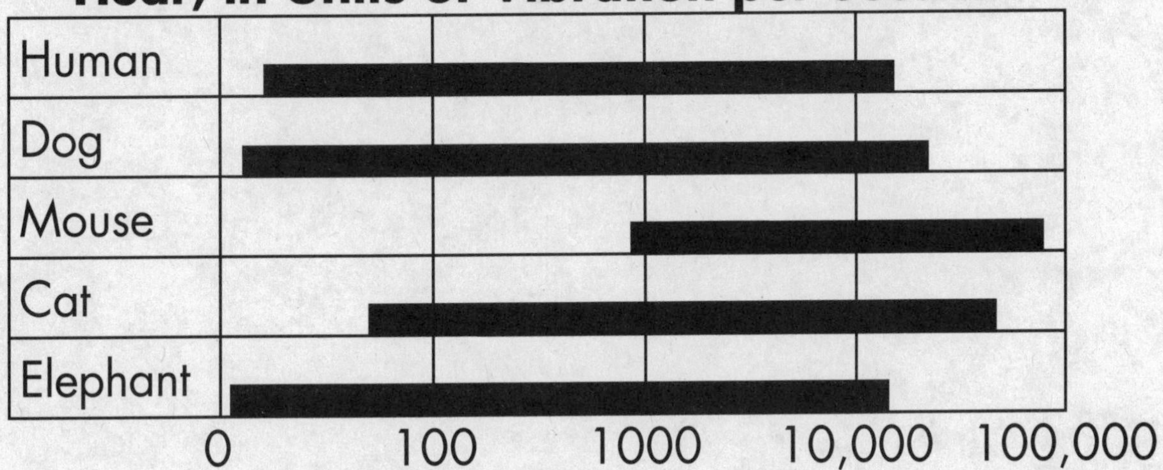

Use the bar graph to answer these questions.

1. Which animal can hear a sound that vibrates almost 100,000 times per second? __________

2. Which animal can hear about the same pitches as humans can hear? __________

3. Which animal can hear sounds with the lowest pitch?

____

Directions: Study the bar graph. Compare the bars. Use the data to help answer the questions.
Home Activity: Your child learned to read a bar graph. With your child, list sounds you can hear in your home. Count how many times you hear each sound in a minute. Make a bar graph with this data. Ask each other questions about your graph.

Notes

Family Science Activity

Make a Paper Cup Telephone

Materials:

- Two paper cups
- Two paper clips
- String
- Scissors
- Pencil

Steps

1. Poke a small hole in the center of each cup's bottom.
2. Cut a piece of string so that it is long enough to cross the widest room in your home.
3. Insert one end of the string through the hole in one cup. Tie the string to a paper clip inside the cup. Repeat with the remaining string and cup.
4. You and your child should each hold a cup. Move away from each other until the string is tight.
5. Take turns speaking into the cup while the other person uses their cup to listen. How does the sound travel?
6. Continue to experiment. What happens when the string is loose? What happens when the string is stretched around a corner? Discuss your observations.

Take Home Booklet

Use with Chapter 11.

Dear Family,

Your child is learning about sound and how sound travels. In the science chapter Sound, our class has learned that sound is made when an object vibrates. The children have also learned about characteristics of sound, such as loudness and pitch.

In addition to learning different ways to describe sound, the children have also learned many new vocabulary words. Help your child to make these words a part of his or her own vocabulary by using them when you talk together about sound.

vibrate
loudness
pitch

The following pages include activities that you and your child can do together. By participating in your child's education, you will help to bring the learning home.

Describe the Sound

Look at the pictures below. Write **LOUD** under the things that make a loud sound. Write **SOFT** under the things that make a soft sound.

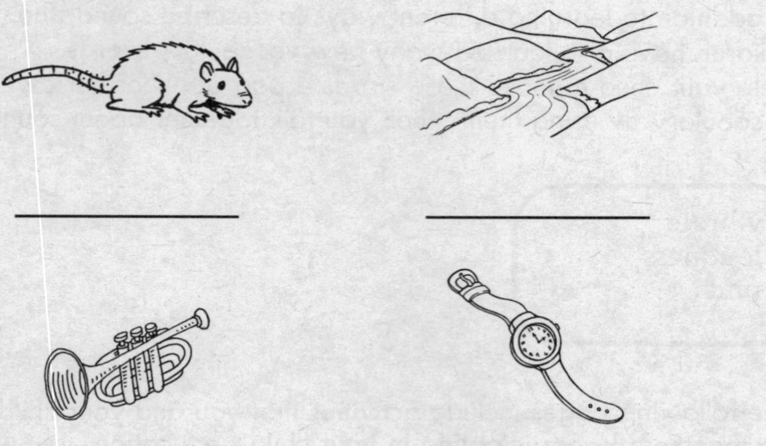

Vocabulary Practice

Draw a line to match each vocabulary word to its definition.

vibrate	how loud or soft a sound is
loudness	how high or low a sound is
pitch	to move quickly back and forth

Fun Fact

The blue whale is the loudest animal on Earth. It can make a sound that is louder than a jet airplane. A blue whale's sound can travel 500 miles through the ocean.

Name ____________________

Draw a picture or write a sentence to go with each word.

solar system	orbit
axis	crater
rotation	phase
constellation	

Directions: Read the words and draw pictures to illustrate them or write sentences about them. Cut out the boxes to use as word cards.
Home Activity: Give clues to the vocabulary words, such as *how Earth goes around the Sun* and *a big hole made by a rock,* and have your child say the correct words.

Name ______________________________

Use with Chapter 12.

Alike and Different

Read the science story.
Look at the pictures.

Spring and Fall

Spring and fall are two seasons of the year. In spring, the days start to get longer. Many trees begin to grow leaves. In fall, the days start to get shorter. The leaves on many trees change color and fall off. But in both seasons, the hours of daylight are about the same.

Apply It!

Fill in the graphic organizer on the next page.
Tell how spring and fall are alike. Tell how they are different.

Name ______________________________

Use with Chapter 12.

Alike

Different

Directions: Read the science story on page 138. Write how spring and fall are alike in the *Alike* box. Write how they are different in the *Different* box.
Home Activity: Your child learned about the concept of alike and different. Display two balls that are different in some ways, such as a baseball and a tennis ball. Ask your child to tell how the balls are alike and how they are different.

Notes

Name ______________________________

Use with pages 367–369.

What is the Sun?

Before You Read Lesson 1

Read each sentence. Do you think it is true? Do you think it is not true? Circle the word or words after each sentence that tell what you think.

1.	The Sun is Earth's closest star.	True	Not True
2.	The Sun is smaller than Earth.	True	Not True
3.	Without the Sun, nothing could live.	True	Not True

After You Read Lesson 1

Read each sentence again. Circle the word or words after each sentence that tell what you think now. Did you change any answers? Put an **X** by each answer that you changed.

1.	The Sun is Earth's closest star.	True	Not True
2.	The Sun is smaller than Earth.	True	Not True
3.	Without the Sun, nothing could live.	True	Not True

Home Activity: Together talk about your child's answers. Have your child explain why his or her answers may have changed after reading the lesson.

Name ______________________________

Use with pages 367–369.

Complete the Sentence

Write the word that completes each sentence.

Sun	star	big	Earth

1. A ______________ is made of hot, glowing gases.
2. The ______________ is the closest star to Earth.
3. The Sun looks small but is very ______________.
4. The Sun is important to ______________.

Important Details

5. Color the things that need light and heat from the Sun.

Name ____________________

Use with pages 370–373.

What causes day and night?

Before You Read Lesson 2

Read each sentence. Do you think it is true? Do you think it is not true? Circle the word or words after each sentence that tell what you think.

1. Half of Earth is always lit by the Sun. True Not True
2. Earth turns once every 24 hours. True Not True
3. The Sun moves across the sky each day. True Not True

After You Read Lesson 2

Read each sentence again. Circle the word or words after each sentence that tell what you think now. Did you change any answers? Put an **X** by each answer that you changed.

1. Half of Earth is always lit by the Sun. True Not True
2. Earth turns once every 24 hours. True Not True
3. The Sun moves across the sky each day. True Not True

Home Activity: Together talk about your child's answers. Have your child explain why his or her answers may have changed after reading the lesson.

Name ______________________________

Use with pages 370–373.

Complete the Sentence

Write the word that completes each sentence.

rotation	axis	day	night

1. Earth turns on an imaginary line called an __________.
2. Every day, Earth makes one ____________, or turn.
3. It is ____________ when your side of Earth faces the Sun.
4. It is ________________ when your side of Earth faces away from the Sun.

Alike and Different

5. How are sunrise and sunset alike? How are they different?

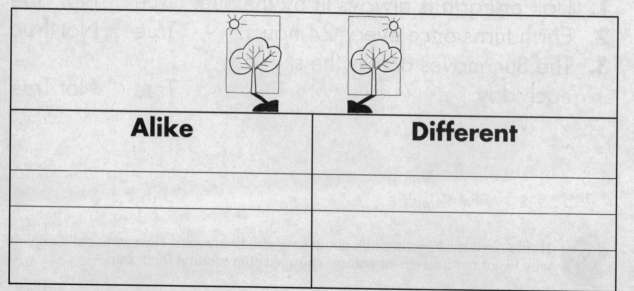

Alike	Different

Name ____________________

Use with pages 374–375.

What causes seasons to change?

Before You Read Lesson 3

Read each sentence. Do you think it is true? Do you think it is not true? Circle the word or words after each sentence that tell what you think.

1. The way Earth spins is called an orbit. True Not True
2. Earth's tilt and Earth's orbit cause the seasons. True Not True
3. We get less direct sunlight in winter. True Not True

After You Read Lesson 3

Read each sentence again. Circle the word or words after each sentence that tell what you think now. Did you change any answers? Put an **X** by each answer that you changed.

1. The way Earth spins is called an orbit. True Not True
2. Earth's tilt and Earth's orbit cause the seasons. True Not True
3. We get less direct sunlight in winter. True Not True

Home Activity: Together talk about your child's answers. Have your child explain why his or her answers may have changed after reading the lesson.

Name ______________________________

Lesson 3 Review

Use with pages 374–375.

Complete the Sentence

Write the word that completes each sentence.

year	orbit	axis	tilted

1. Earth is always ______________ in the same direction.

2. Earth spins on its ______________.

3. Earth makes one ______________ around the Sun every year.

4. Earth orbits the Sun one time in a ______________.

Infer

5. Draw the Sun where it would be when we are in summer.

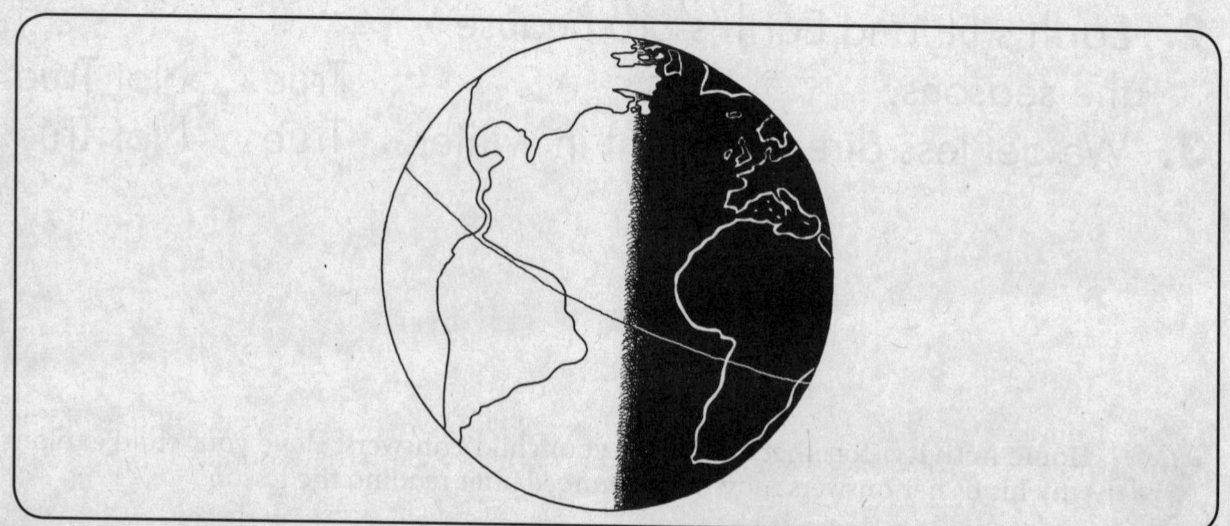

Name ________________________________

Use with pages 376–379.

What can you see in the night sky?

Before You Read Lesson 4

Read each sentence. Do you think it is true? Do you think it is not true? Circle the word or words after each sentence that tell what you think.

1.	Patterns of stars are constellations.	True	Not True
2.	The Moon has a smooth surface.	True	Not True
3.	The Moon can be seen in the daytime.	True	Not True

After You Read Lesson 4

Read each sentence again. Circle the word or words after each sentence that tell what you think now. Did you change any answers? Put an **X** by each answer that you changed.

1.	Patterns of stars are constellations.	True	Not True
2.	The Moon has a smooth surface.	True	Not True
3.	The Moon can be seen in the daytime.	True	Not True

Home Activity: Together talk about your child's answers. Have your child explain why his or her answers may have changed after reading the lesson.

Name ________________________________

Use with pages 376–379.

Complete the Sentence

Write the word that completes each sentence.

small	Moon	crater	constellation

1. The largest thing you can see in the night sky is the ________________.

2. Stars in the night sky look ________________ because they are far away.

3. A ________________ is a bowl-shaped hole in the ground.

4. A ________________ is a group of stars that form a picture.

Picture Clues

5. What do you see? Connect the stars to form a constellation and name it.

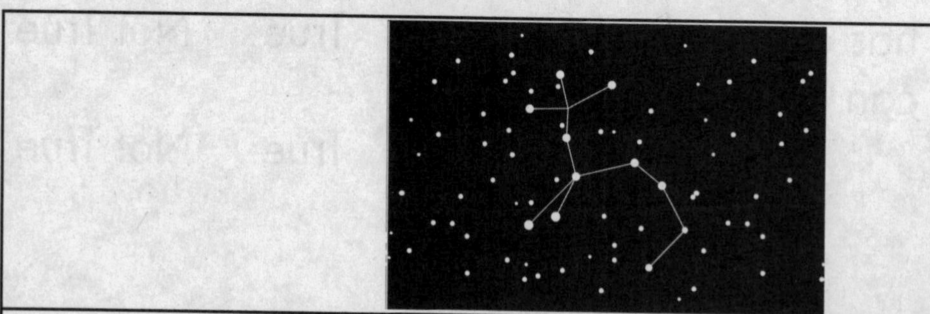

I would name my constellation:

____

Name ______________________________

Use with pages 380–381.

Why does the Moon seem to change?

Before You Read Lesson 5

Read each sentence. Do you think it is true? Do you think it is not true? Circle the word or words after each sentence that tell what you think.

1.	The Moon orbits Earth.	True	Not True
2.	The Moon makes its own light.	True	Not True
3.	Phases of the Moon have different shapes.	True	Not True

After You Read Lesson 5

Read each sentence again. Circle the word or words after each sentence that tell what you think now. Did you change any answers? Put an **X** by each answer that you changed.

1.	The Moon orbits Earth.	True	Not True
2.	The Moon makes its own light.	True	Not True
3.	Phases of the Moon have different shapes.	True	Not True

Home Activity: Together talk about your child's answers. Have your child explain why his or her answers may have changed after reading the lesson.

Name ______________________________

Lesson 5 Review

Use with pages 380–381.

Complete the Sentence

Write the word that completes each sentence.

four	phase	light	rotates

1. The Moon ______________, or turns, as it goes around Earth.

2. The Moon does not make its own ______________.

3. It takes about ______________ weeks for the Moon to move around Earth.

4. A ______________ is the shape of the lighted part of the Moon.

Alike and Different

5. How are the Sun and the Moon alike? How are they different?

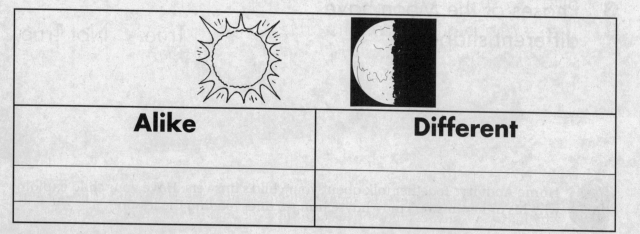

Alike	Different

Name ______________________________

Use with pages 382–383.

What is the solar system?

Before You Read Lesson 6

Read each sentence. Do you think it is true? Do you think it is not true? Circle the word or words after each sentence that tell what you think.

1. Only planets are in our solar system.	True	Not True
2. The Sun is the center of our solar system.	True	Not True
3. There are nine planets in our solar system.	True	Not True

After You Read Lesson 6

Read each sentence again. Circle the word or words after each sentence that tell what you think now. Did you change any answers? Put an **X** by each answer that you changed.

1. Only planets are in our solar system.	True	Not True
2. The Sun is the center of our solar system.	True	Not True
3. There are nine planets in our solar system.	True	Not True

Home Activity: Together talk about your child's answers. Have your child explain why his or her answers may have changed after reading the lesson.

Name ______________________

Use with pages 382–383.

Complete the Sentence

Write the word phrase that completes each sentence.

planet	Sun	orbit	solar system

1. Planets ______________ around the Sun.

2. The center of our solar system is the ______________.

3. The planets, moons, stars, and Sun make up our ______________.

4. Earth is the third ______________ from the Sun.

Important Details

5. Label Earth. Can you label any of the other planets?

Name ______________________

Use with Chapter 12.

Amount of Daylight and the Seasons

The amount of daylight we get changes with the seasons. The table shows how many hours and minutes of daylight we had on the first day of each season in 2004.

Amount of Daylight on the First Day of Each Season

Season–First Day	Hours and Minutes of Daylight
Spring—March 21	12 hours, 13 minutes
Summer—June 21	15 hours, 13 minutes
Fall—September 21	12 hours, 11 minutes
Winter—December 21	8 hours, 8 minutes

Data from U.S. Navy for 2004

Use the information in the table to answer the questions.

1. Which first day had the least hours and minutes of daylight? ______________
2. Which first day had the most hours and minutes of daylight? ______________
3. In which first days were the hours of daylight and darkness about the same? ______________________

Directions: Read the table. Compare the hours and minutes in the second column. Use the information to answer the questions.

Home Activity: Your child learned to read a table. Find a table in a newspaper or magazine. Discuss what information the table gives and how it is organized. Then ask questions that require your child to find information in the table.

Notes

Family Science Activity

A Moon Journal

Materials:

- Nine sheets of drawing paper
- Construction paper
- Crayons or markers
- Stapler
- A pencil or pen

Steps

1. Make a Moon journal with your child. Draw a line across the middle of the pages (on both sides) to create two equal halves. Have your child make a cover out of construction paper. Staple the booklet together along the long edge.
2. Talk about the changing phases of the Moon. The Moon reflects light from the Sun. We only see the part of the Moon that the Sun shines on. Talk about why the Moon seems to change shape.
3. Every night for the next four weeks, have your child find the Moon in the sky and make a drawing of it, starting on the top half of the first page of the booklet. Have your child write the time and date of observation below each drawing.
4. If it is rainy or cloudy, have your child record that on the page for that date.
5. After 32 days, look at the drawings your child made of the Moon. Talk with your child about the different shapes the Moon had during this time. Figure out how long it takes for the Moon to go through one cycle. Check your calculation against a calendar or newspaper that shows the phases of the Moon.

Dear Family,

Your child is learning how Earth, the Sun, and the Moon move. In the science chapter Earth and Space, our class has learned that Earth's movement causes day and night and the change of seasons. The children have also learned about the Moon and the rest of the solar system.

In addition to learning what is in the day and night sky, the children have also learned many new vocabulary words. Help your child to make these words a part of his or her own vocabulary by using them when you talk together about Earth, the Sun, and the Moon.

axis
rotation
orbit
constellation
crater
phase
solar system

These following pages include activities that you and your child can do together. By participating in your child's education, you will help to bring the learning home.

Star Picture

Draw a picture of the Big Dipper in the box below. First draw the stars with a pencil. Then connect the stars to show the constellation. Write the name of the constellation on the line.

____

Vocabulary Practice

The letters of each word below are all mixed up. Look at each group of letters. Decide what vocabulary word the letters spell. Then, write the word on the line. If you need help, look at the vocabulary words in the box below.

1. TATROINO _______
2. SIXA _______
3. RITOB _______
4. RECTRA _______
5. LATICTSONELON _______
6. HEAPS _______

axis
crater
rotation
constellation
orbit
phase

Name ______________________

Vocabulary Preview

Use with Chapter 13.

Draw a picture or write a sentence to go with each word.

technology	invent
transportation	engine
vaccine	satellite
meteorologist	manufacture

Directions: Read the words and draw pictures to illustrate them or write sentences about them. Cut out the boxes to use as word cards.
Home Activity: Give your child clues about each word, such as *This person gives the weather forecast* and *It changes gasoline into energy for moving.* Have your child name the correct vocabulary term.

Name ____________________

Use with Chapter 13.

Retell

Read the science article.

Telephones
The telephone was invented in 1876. It made sound travel through a wire using electricity. In 1973, the first public call was made on a cell phone. It used radio signals and had no wires.

Apply It!

What did you learn about telephones? Tell it in your own words. Use the space on the next page.

Name ____________________

Retell

Directions: Read the Science Article and look at the pictures. Then tell about what you learned. Use your own words.

Home Activity: Your child learned about retelling. Together, read a short newspaper or magazine article. Then ask your child to tell you about what he or she learned by reading.

Notes

Name ______________________________

Use with pages 399–401.

What is technology?

Before You Read Lesson 1

Read each sentence. Do you think it is true? Do you think it is not true? Circle the word or words after each sentence that tell what you think.

1.	People use technology to solve problems.	True	Not True
2.	Gasoline adds pollution to the air.	True	Not True
3.	Today people use steam engines.	True	Not True

After You Read Lesson 1

Read each sentence again. Circle the word or words after each sentence that tell what you think now. Did you change any answers? Put an **X** by each answer that you changed.

1.	People use technology to solve problems.	True	Not True
2.	Gasoline adds pollution to the air.	True	Not True
3.	Today people use steam engines.	True	Not True

Home Activity: Together talk about your child's answers. Have your child explain why his or her answers may have changed after reading the lesson.

Name ______________________

Use with pages 399–401.

Complete the Sentence

Write the word that completes each sentence.

invent	technology	transportation	engine

1. Using science to help us solve problems is called ______________.
2. To ______________ is to make something new.
3. The way we move from place to place is called ______________.
4. A machine that does work or makes something move is an ______________.

Retell

5. What inventions did you read about that have made transportation easier? How did they do it?

Retell

____

____

____

____

Name ______________________________

Use with pages 402–403.

How does technology help us?

Before You Read Lesson 2

Read each sentence. Do you think it is true? Do you think it is not true? Circle the word or words after each sentence that tell what you think.

1.	Doctors use technology to help people.	True	Not True
2.	A vaccine can cure a disease.	True	Not True
3.	Doctors use X-rays to see inside people.	True	Not True

After You Read Lesson 2

Read each sentence again. Circle the word or words after each sentence that tell what you think now. Did you change any answers? Put an **X** by each answer that you changed.

1.	Doctors use technology to help people.	True	Not True
2.	A vaccine can cure a disease.	True	Not True
3.	Doctors use X-rays to see inside people.	True	Not True

Home Activity: Together talk about your child's answers. Have your child explain why his or her answers may have changed after reading the lesson.

Name ______________________________

Use with pages 402–403.

Complete the Sentence

Write the word that completes each sentence.

vaccine	problems	artificial	X-rays

1. A medicine that can prevent a disease is a ______________.

2. Something that is ______________ is fake or not real.

3. ______________ help doctors see inside us.

4. Technology uses science to solve ______________.

Retell

5. Why do doctors need to know what is wrong with us?

Retell

Name ____________________

Use with pages 404–405.

How do we use technology to communicate?

Before You Read Lesson 3

Read each sentence. Do you think it is true? Do you think it is not true? Circle the word or words after each sentence that tell what you think.

1. We use computers to communicate. True Not True

2. Communication technology has changed a lot. True Not True

3. Astronauts use telephones to send messages from space. True Not True

After You Read Lesson 3

Read each sentence again. Circle the word or words after each sentence that tell what you think now. Did you change any answers? Put an **X** by each answer that you changed.

1. We use computers to communicate. True Not True

2. Communication technology has changed a lot. True Not True

3. Astronauts use telephones to send messages from space. True Not True

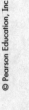

Home Activity: Together talk about your child's answers. Have your child explain why his or her answers may have changed after reading the lesson.

Name ______________________________

Use with pages 404–405.

Complete the Sentence

Write the word that completes each sentence.

telephone	computer	messages	communicate

1. We use telephones and computers to ____________, or talk to other people.

2. Computers let us send ______________ to our friends.

3. The ______________ was invented in 1876.

4. The ______________ was invented in 1946.

Infer

5. Color the pictures that show technology that helps us communicate.

Name ______________________________

Use with pages 406–407.

What are some other ways we use technology?

Before You Read Lesson 4

Read each sentence. Do you think it is true? Do you think it is not true? Circle the word or words after each sentence that tell what you think.

1.	Technology makes our lives harder.	True	Not True
2.	Technology helps people at work.	True	Not True
3.	Satellites help show weather patterns.	True	Not True

After You Read Lesson 4

Read each sentence again. Circle the word or words after each sentence that tell what you think now. Did you change any answers? Put an **X** by each answer that you changed.

1.	Technology makes our lives harder.	True	Not True
2.	Technology helps people at work.	True	Not True
3.	Satellites help show weather patterns.	True	Not True

Home Activity: Together talk about your child's answers. Have your child explain why his or her answers may have changed after reading the lesson.

Name ______________________________

Lesson 4 Review

Use with pages 406–407.

Complete the Sentence

Write the word that completes each sentence.

satellite	music	math	meteorologist

1. People listen to ____________ on compact discs.

2. People use calculators to do ____________.

3. A ____________ studies weather.

4. A ____________ revolves around another object, such as Earth.

Retell

5. How does technology help us have fun?

Retell

Name ________________________

Think, Read, Learn

Use with pages 408–409.

How do people make things?

Before You Read Lesson 5

Read each sentence. Do you think it is true? Do you think it is not true? Circle the word or words after each sentence that tell what you think.

1.	Wool is a natural material.	True	Not True
2.	Manufactured things are made only by machine.	True	Not True
3.	Plastic is made by people.	True	Not True

After You Read Lesson 5

Read each sentence again. Circle the word or words after each sentence that tell what you think now. Did you change any answers? Put an **X** by each answer that you changed.

1.	Wool is a natural material.	True	Not True
2.	Manufactured things are made only by machine.	True	Not True
3.	Plastic is made by people.	True	Not True

Home Activity: Together talk about your child's answers. Have your child explain why his or her answers may have changed after reading the lesson.

Name ______________________________

Use with pages 408–409.

Complete the Sentence

Write the word that completes each sentence.

wool	materials	rubber	manufacture

1. To ____________ is to make something with machines or by hand.

2. Some ____________ come from nature.

3. Some items are made from ____________, which comes from sheep.

4. Bike tires are made from ____________.

Alike and Different

5. How are the materials that make a shirt and a tricycle alike? How are they different?

Alike	Different

Name ________________________

Use with Chapter 13.

Record and Use Data

Gina asked these questions:
Does your family have a computer?
Does your family have a cell phone?
This is what she found.

Technology at Home	
Families that have a computer at home	卌 卌 |
Families that have a cell phone	卌 卌 卌

Use the chart to answer the questions.

1. How many of Gina's classmates have a computer at home? ________

2. How many of these families have a cell phone?

____

3. How many more families have cell phones than computers? Write a number sentence.

____

Directions: Look at the table. Count how many families have computers and cell phones. Use those numbers to answer the questions.
Home Activity: Your child learned about using a data table. With your child, count the inventions in your home that help with food storage and preparation. Make a data table like the one on the page. Ask your child to make a number sentence using the data.

Notes

Family Science Activity

Manufacture a Collage

Materials:
- Large sheet of drawing paper or oak tag
- Magazines
- Scissors
- Paste
- Pencil or pen

Steps

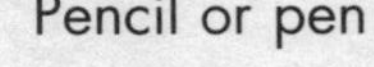

1. People manufacture things we use every day. Remind your child that manufacture means to make by hand or by machines. Encourage your child to think about the manufactured goods he or she uses on a daily basis.
2. Then, look through magazines and cut out pictures of these manufactured items.
3. Organize the manufactured items into groups. Help your child determine whether the manufactured items are made of natural materials, such as wool; man-made materials, like plastic; or a combination of both.
4. Make a technology collage by pasting the pictures onto the drawing paper or oak tag.
5. Entitle the collage and each category. Help your child label each picture.
6. Encourage your child to show the collage to friends and family. Prompt them to discuss their use of manufactured items.

Take Home Booklet

Use with Chapter 13.

Dear Family,

Your child is learning how technology has changed the world. In the science chapter Technology in Our World, our class has learned how technology shapes many aspects of our daily lives, including transportation, medicine, communication, and entertainment. The children have also learned how people manufacture objects and materials, by hand and with machines.

In addition to learning how technology has helped us solve problems, the children have also learned many new vocabulary words. Help your child to make these words a part of his or her own vocabulary by using them when you talk together about technology.

technology
invent
transportation
engine
vaccine
meteorologist
satellite
manufacture

The following pages include activities that you and your child can do together. By participating in your child's education, you will help to bring the learning home.

Transportation Drawing

Invent something that will help you at home. What does your invention do? How does it work? Draw a picture of your invention in the box. Write two sentences that tell about your invention.

Vocabulary Practice

Read each clue. Then, write the vocabulary word in the box.

1 A machine that does work or makes something move

				n	

2 Using science to help us solve problems

	c								

3 To make something for the first time

				n	

4 The way people or things move from place to place

	r												

5 To make by hand or by machines

				f						

Name ____________________________

Use with Chapter 1, pp. 23, 25.

How are plants different in the desert and marsh?

Some plants live in the desert. A desert is very dry. Plants that live in the desert can hold water. Some plants live in the marsh. The soil in a marsh may not have nutrients plants need. Some plants that live in a marsh catch insects for food.

Desert

The **saguaro cactus** has a long stem that holds water.

Marsh

A **Venus's-flytrap** catches insects with its leaves.

Please answer the questions.

1. Which plant lives in the desert?

____

2. Which plant lives in the marsh?

____

3. Which plant holds water?

____

4. A saguaro cactus has a long ________.

5. A Venus's-flytrap catches insects with its ________.

Name ____________________

Use with Chapter 2, pp. 40–41.

Which animals have backbones?

There are two main large groups of animals. One large group does not have backbones. Insects and spiders are in this group. The other large group has backbones. This group includes five smaller groups.

Groups of Animals with Backbones

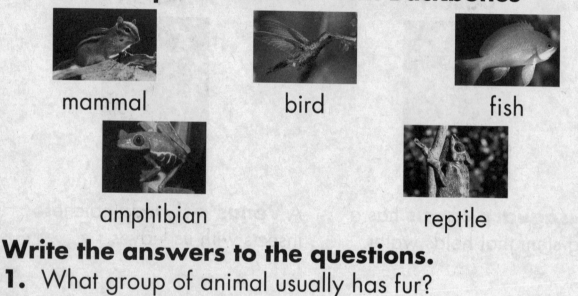

mammal

bird

fish

amphibian

reptile

Write the answers to the questions.

1. What group of animal usually has fur?

   ____

2. What group of animal lives in the water and has fins?

   ____

3. What group of animal has wings?

   ____

4. Name at least one way a mammal is different from a fish.

   ____

Name ______________________________

Use with Chapter 3, pp. 74–75.

What is a food chain?

Living things need food. Plants use energy from sunlight to make food. Some animals eat plants. Other animals eat those animals. That is a food chain. Animals that eat other animals are called predators. The animals they eat are called prey.

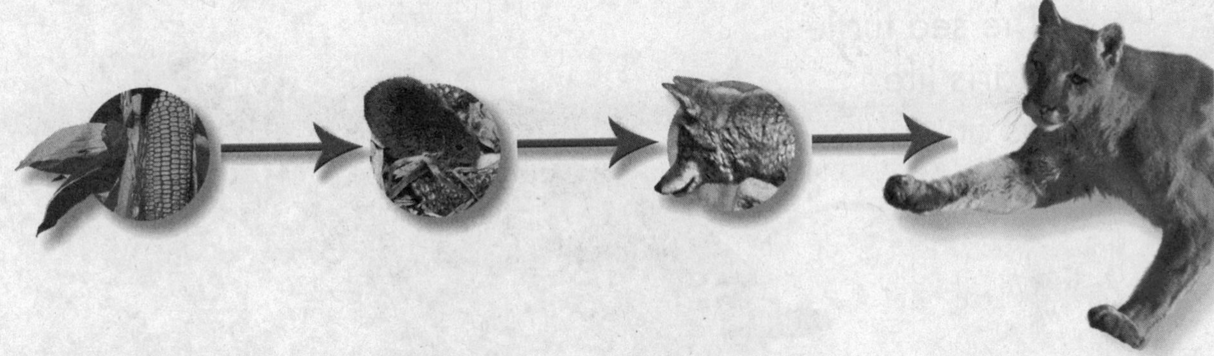

The corn plant uses water, air, and sunlight to make food.

The vole eats the corn.

The coyote eats the vole.

The mountain lion eats the coyote.

Answer these questions.

1. How many animals are in this food chain?

____

2. What plant is in this food chain?

____

3. What animal does the coyote eat?

____

4. The vole is the ________ of the coyote.
5. The mountain lion is the coyote's ________.

Name ______________________________

Using Science Pictures

Use with Chapter 4, pp. 106–107.

What is the life cycle of a sea turtle?

The way a living thing grows and changes is called its life cycle. These pictures show the life cycle of a sea turtle.

The sea turtle starts life as an egg.
One day the adult sea turtle may have young turtles of its own.
A young sea turtle comes out of the egg.

Answer these questions.

1. The way a living thing grows and changes is its ________.
2. What comes out of the sea turtle's egg?

   ____
3. The sea turtle starts life as an ________.
4. One day the sea turtle may have young ________.

Name ______________________

Use with Chapter 5, pp. 148–149.

What are different kinds of soil?

Most land is covered with soil. Soil has air and water. Many kinds of soil have sand, clay, and humus in them. Most plants need soil to grow. People need soil to grow plants for food. Different kinds of plants grow in different kinds of soil.

Sandy Soil

Sandy soil feels dry and rough. There is sandy soil in deserts.

Clay Soil

Clay soil has very small pieces. It feels soft and sticky.

Humus

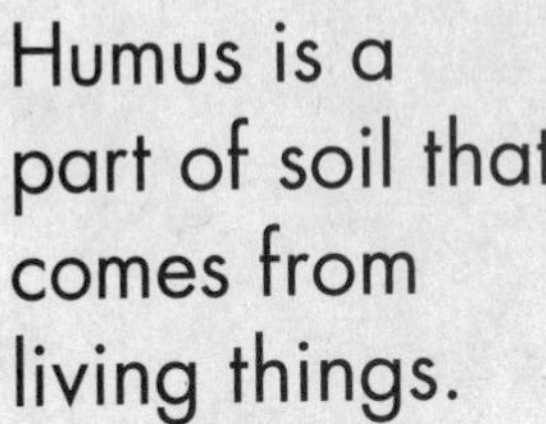

Humus is a part of soil that comes from living things.

Answer these questions.

1. What kind of soil is dry?

____

2. What kind of soil feels sticky and soft?

____

3. What part of soil comes from living things?

____

4. Which kind of soil has more water, clay soil or sandy soil?

____

Name ______________________________

Use with Chapter 6, pp. 178–179.

What is the water cycle?

Water moves from the clouds to Earth and back to the clouds again. This is called the water cycle. The water cycle never stops.

When water vapor in clouds gets cold, it condenses. This means it changes into tiny drops of water. The drops form clouds. Then the cycle begins again.

Water falls from clouds. It might be rain, snow, hail or sleet.

Energy from the Sun makes some of the water evaporate and change to water vapor. You cannot see water vapor.

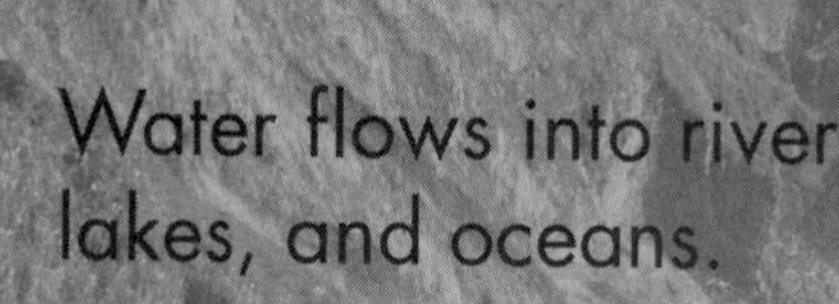

Water flows into rivers, lakes, and oceans.

Answer these questions.

1. What does rain fall from?

____

2. Where does water go when it falls to Earth?

____

3. What happens to water when it evaporates?

____

4. __________ are made of tiny drops of water.

Name ______________________

Using Science Pictures

Use with Chapter 7, pp. 209.

How is a fossil formed?

A fossil shows the shape of a plant or animal that lived long ago. Fossils can tell us about plants and animals that do not live on Earth any more.

A Fossil Is Formed.

A lizard dies.

The lizard is covered by sand and mud.

The sand and mud become rock with a fossil that shows us the shape of the lizard.

Answer these questions.

1. What animal becomes a fossil in these pictures?

____

2. Is the lizard alive when it starts to become a fossil?

____

3. What happens to the sand and mud that cover the lizard?

____

Name ______________________________

Use with Chapter 8, pp. 251.

What are some mixtures with water?

A mixture is made of two or more things that do not change. Some mixtures are made with water. There are different ways to separate these mixtures. One way is to let the matter sink. Another way is to let the water evaporate.

Sand and Water

It is easy to see the sand and the water in this mixture.

Salt and Water

The cup on the left is a mixture of salt and water. Look at the cup on the right. The water evaporated. Now it is easy to see the salt.

Answer these questions.

1. Which is heavier, sand or water?

____

2. What is one way to separate salt and water?

____

3. What happens after sand and water are mixed?

____

4. These mixtures both have __________ in them.

Name ________________________________

Use with Chapter 9, pp. 280–281.

How does heat move?

Heat moves from warmer objects to cooler objects. The pan in the picture is metal. Metal is a conductor. Heat can easily move from a stove through the metal. Cloth and wood are not good conductors. The cooking mitt in the picture is made of cloth. It helps keep hands safe from the heat of the pan.

Answer these questions about heat.

1. Heat moves from ________ objects to ________ objects.

2. Metal is a good ________ of heat.

3. The pan is made of ________.

4. ________ and ________ are not good conductors of heat.

Name ______________________

Use with Chapter 10, pp. 314–315.

What are some simple machines?

A simple machine is a tool that can do work. Simple machines have a few or no moving parts. There are six kinds of simple machines.

Wedge

Screw

Lever

Inclined plane

Wheel and Axle

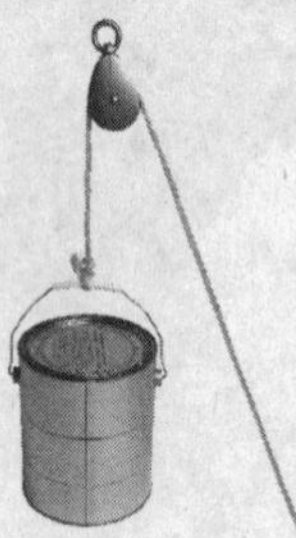

Pulley

Complete the sentences.

1. A ________ ________ is a tool.
2. Simple machines have a few or no ________ parts.
3. A simple machine can do ________.
4. There are ________ kinds of simple machines.

Name ______________________________

Use with Chapter 11, pp. 338–339.

What is pitch?

Pitch describes how high or low a sound is. When you blow across a bottle, the air inside vibrates. Bottles with a lot of air make sounds with a low pitch. Bottles with only a little air make sounds with a high pitch.

1 2 3 4

Answer these questions about pitch.

1. What is pitch?

____

2. What vibrates when you blow across a bottle? __________.

3. Which bottle would have the highest pitch? __________.

4. Which bottle would have the lowest pitch? __________.

Name ______________________

Use with Chapter 12, pp. 382–383.

What is the solar system?

Earth is a planet. It orbits around the Sun. Other planets also orbit around the Sun. The planets and their moons and other objects that orbit around the Sun are called the solar system.

Answer these questions.

1. The largest planet in the solar system is ________.
2. ________ is the planet closest to the Sun.
3. The planet ________ is farthest from the Sun.
4. The planets that are closer to the Sun than Earth are ________ and ________.
5. ________ is the third planet from the Sun.

Name ____________________

Use with Chapter 13, pp. 400–401.

What are some changes in transportation?

Long ago, steam engines made trains and boats move. Today, trains, cars, and boats have electric or gasoline engines. Now, people can travel faster and farther than they did before.

Answer these questions.

1. Long ago, trains had ________ engines.
2. Today, cars have ________ or electric engines.
3. What other kind of transportation has gasoline engines? ________________.
4. Now, people can travel ________ and farther than before.

Notes